IMAGE COMICS, INC. • **Robert Kirkman**: Chief Operating Officer • **Erik Larsen**: Chief Financial Officer • **Todd McFarlane**: President • **Marc Silvestri**: Chief Executive Officer • **Jim Valentino**: Vice President • **Eric Stephenson**: Publisher / Chief Creative Officer • **Corey Hart**: Director of Sales • **Jeff Boison**: Director of Publishing Planning & Book Trade Sales • **Chris Ross**: Director of Digital Sales • **Jeff Stang**: Director of Specialty Sales • **Kat Salazar**: Director of PR & Marketing • **Drew Gill**: Art Director • **Heather Doornink**: Production Director • **Nicole Lapalme**: Controller • **IMAGECOMICS.COM**

EAST OF WEST, VOLUME 8. August 2018. Copyright © 2018 Jonathan Hickman & Nick Dragotta. All rights reserved. Published by Image Comics, Inc. Office of publication: 2701 NW Vaughn St., Suite 780, Portland, OR 97210. Contains material originally published in single magazine form as EAST OF WEST #35-38. "East of West," its logo, and the likenesses of all characters herein are trademarks of Jonathan Hickman & Nick Dragotta, unless otherwise noted. Image Comics logos are registered trademarks of Image Comics, Inc. No part of this publication may be reproduced or transmitted, in any form or by any means (except for short excerpts for review purposes), without the express written permission of Jonathan Hickman & Nick Dragotta, or Image Comics, Inc. All names, characters, events and locales in this publication are entirely fictional. Any resemblance to actual persons (living or dead), events or places, without satiric intent, is coincidental. Printed in the USA. For information regarding the CPSIA on this printed material call: 203-595-3636 and provide reference #RICH–808032. For international rights, contact: foreignlicensing@imagecomics.com. ISBN: 978-1-5343-0556-4.

EAST OF WEST

JONATHAN HICKMAN
WRITER

NICK DRAGOTTA
ARTIST

FRANK MARTIN
COLORS

RUS WOOTON
LETTERS

EAS

W

T

OF

EST

IF YOU CHOOSE, **CHOOSE NOW.**

OR **SOON** THAT DECISION WILL BE **TAKEN FROM YOU.**

The edge of war.

Feel that? The air is supercharged with violence.

If a decision needs to be made...then we must make it *soon.*

I think we're running out of time.

Oh, we definitely are. The war to end all wars is headed towards us like a freight train...

I can almost see it just over the horizon. This *should be our time,* but we're rudderless and without purpose.

Adrift on a bloody sea.

Speak for yourself, War. I don't need convincing...

I know what we're supposed to be doing. *It's simple.* He's the *real thing...*

We need to find the boy, *Babylon,* and serve him.

I'm not so sure...

I am.

Mankind is waiting for *him...*

And *he* is waiting for *us.*

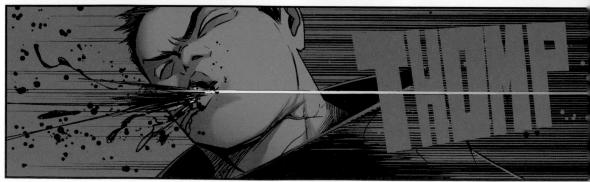

THUMP

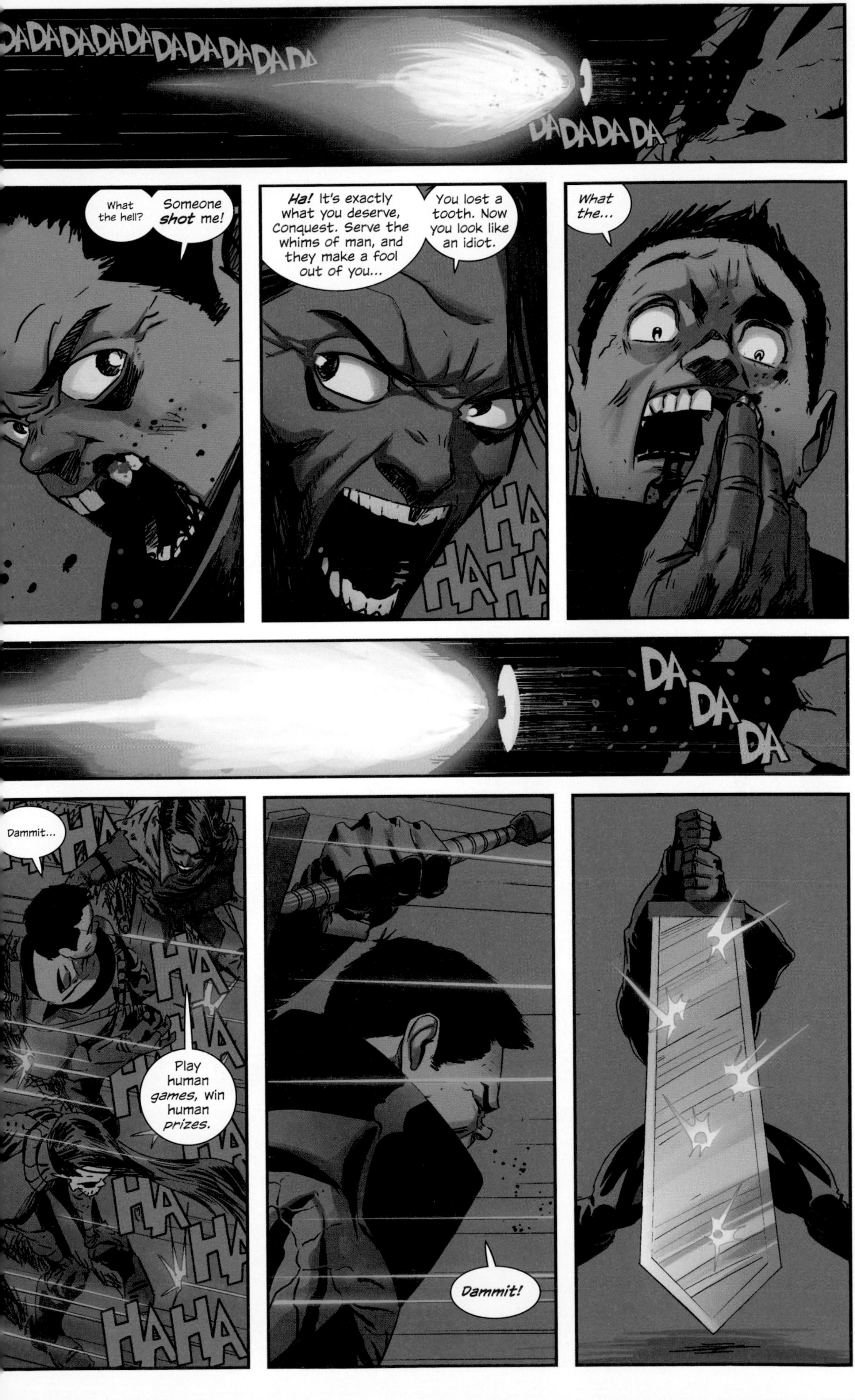
DADADADADADADADADADADA
DADADADA
What the hell?
Someone *shot* me!
Ha! It's exactly what you deserve, Conquest. Serve the whims of man, and they make a fool out of you...
You lost a tooth. Now you look like an idiot.
HAHAHA
What the...
DA DA DA
Dammit...
HAHAHA
Play human *games*, win human *prizes.*
HAHAHAHA
Dammit!

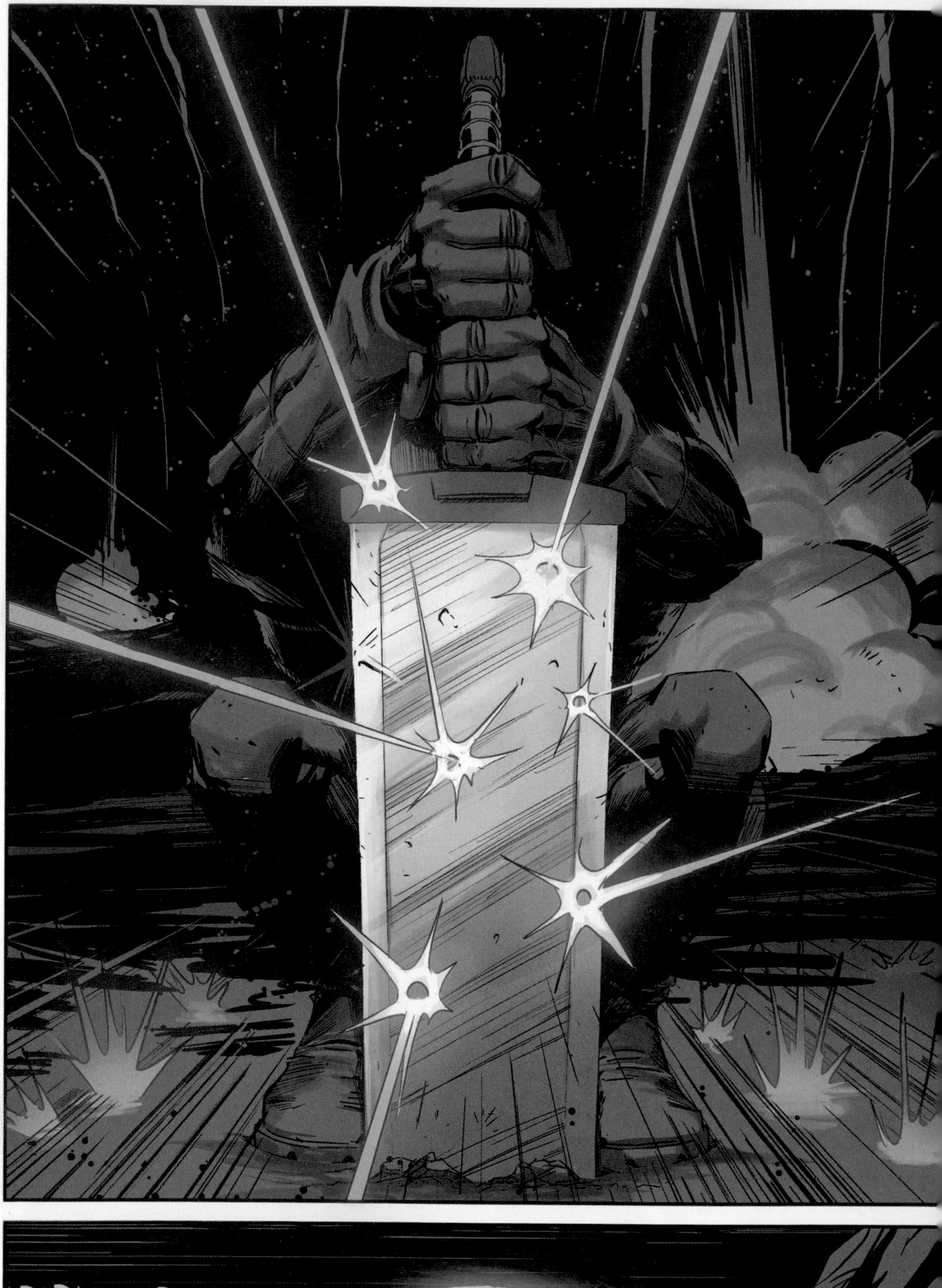

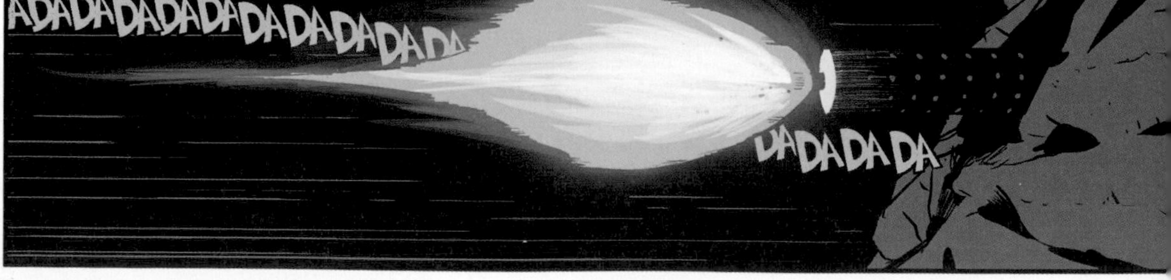
ADADADADADADADADADADA
DADADADA

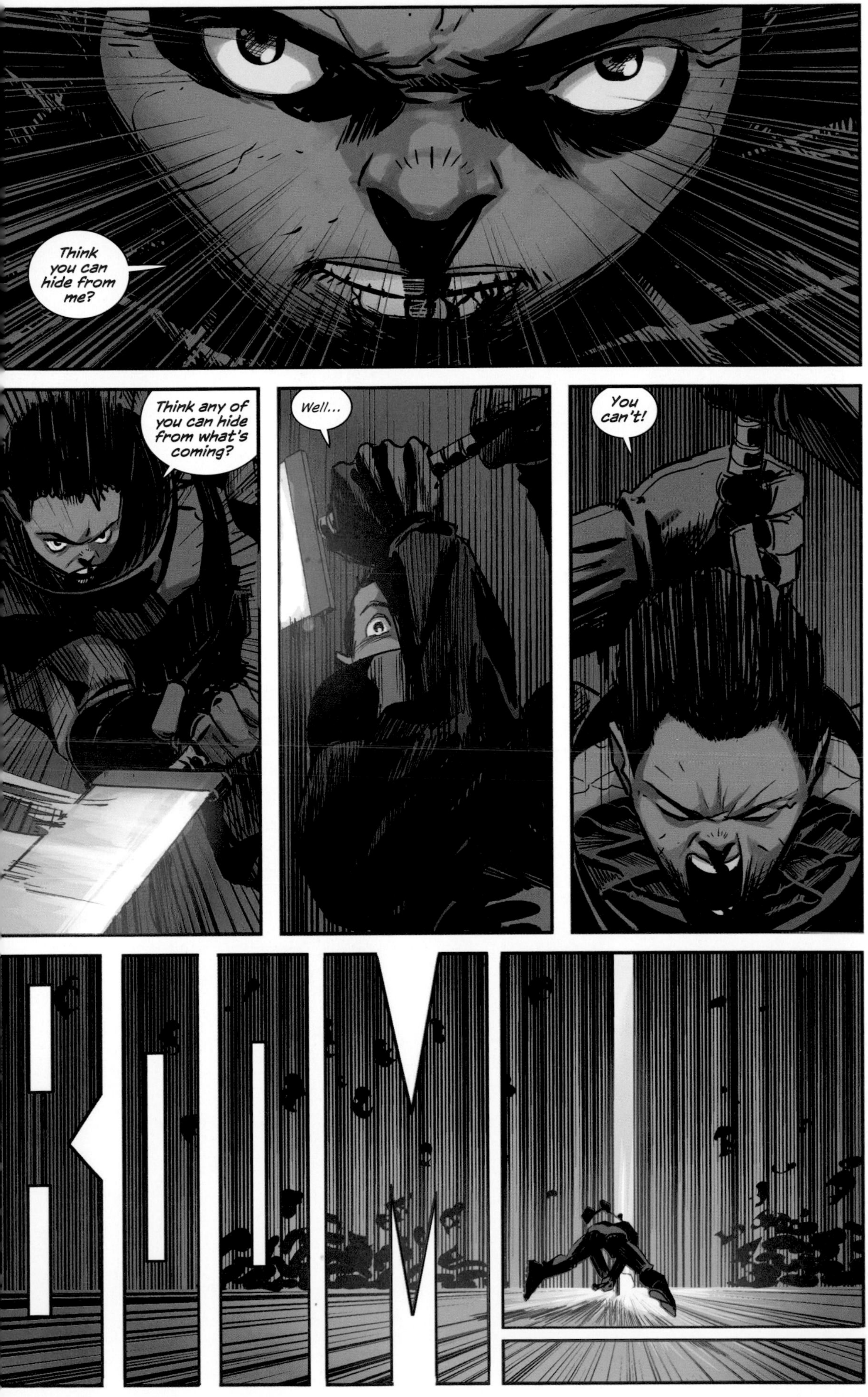
Think you can hide from me?
Think any of you can hide from what's coming?
Well...
You can't!
BOOM!

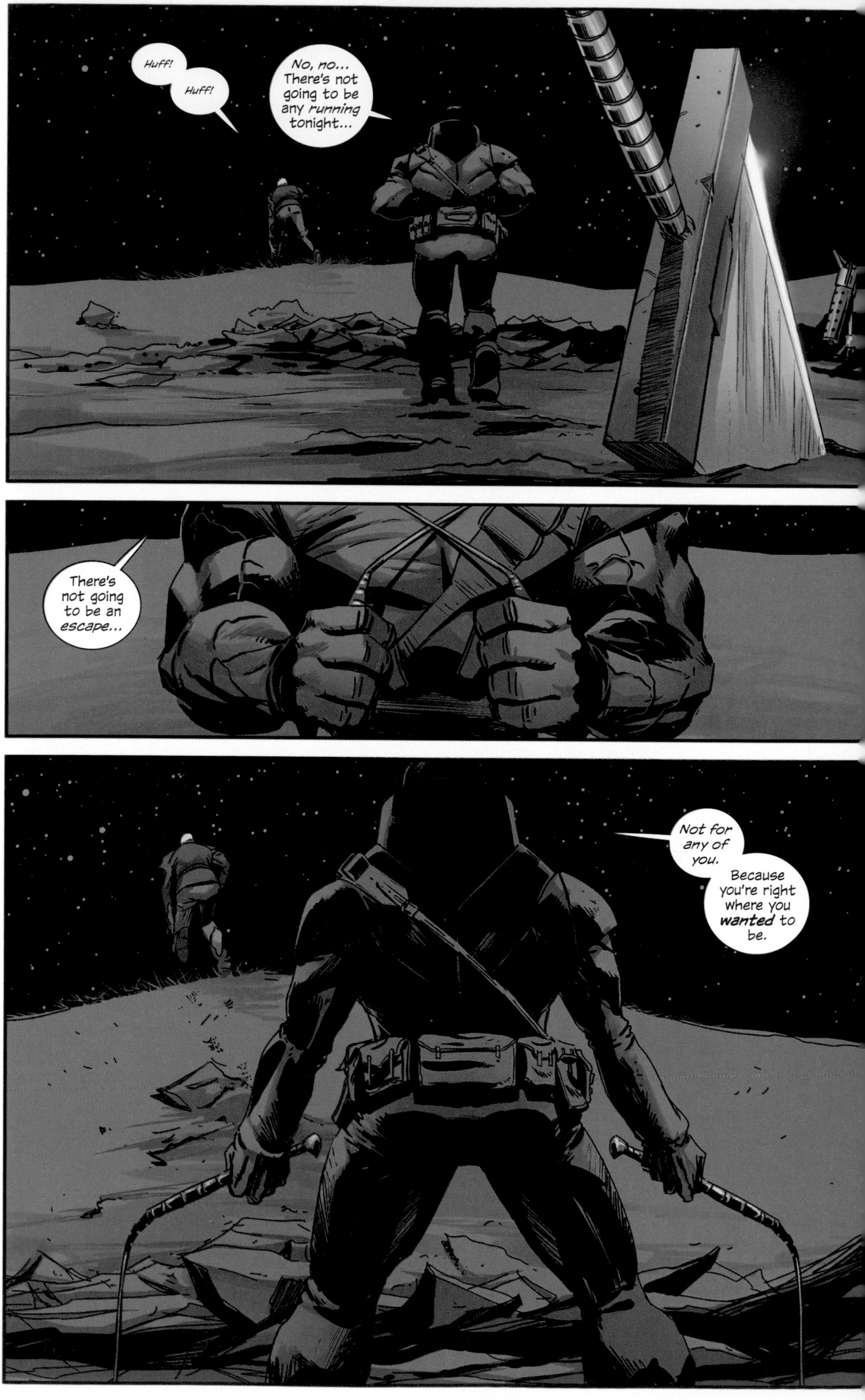
Huff!
Huff!
No, no... There's not going to be any *running* tonight...
There's not going to be an *escape*...
Not for any of you.
Because you're right where you ***wanted*** to be.

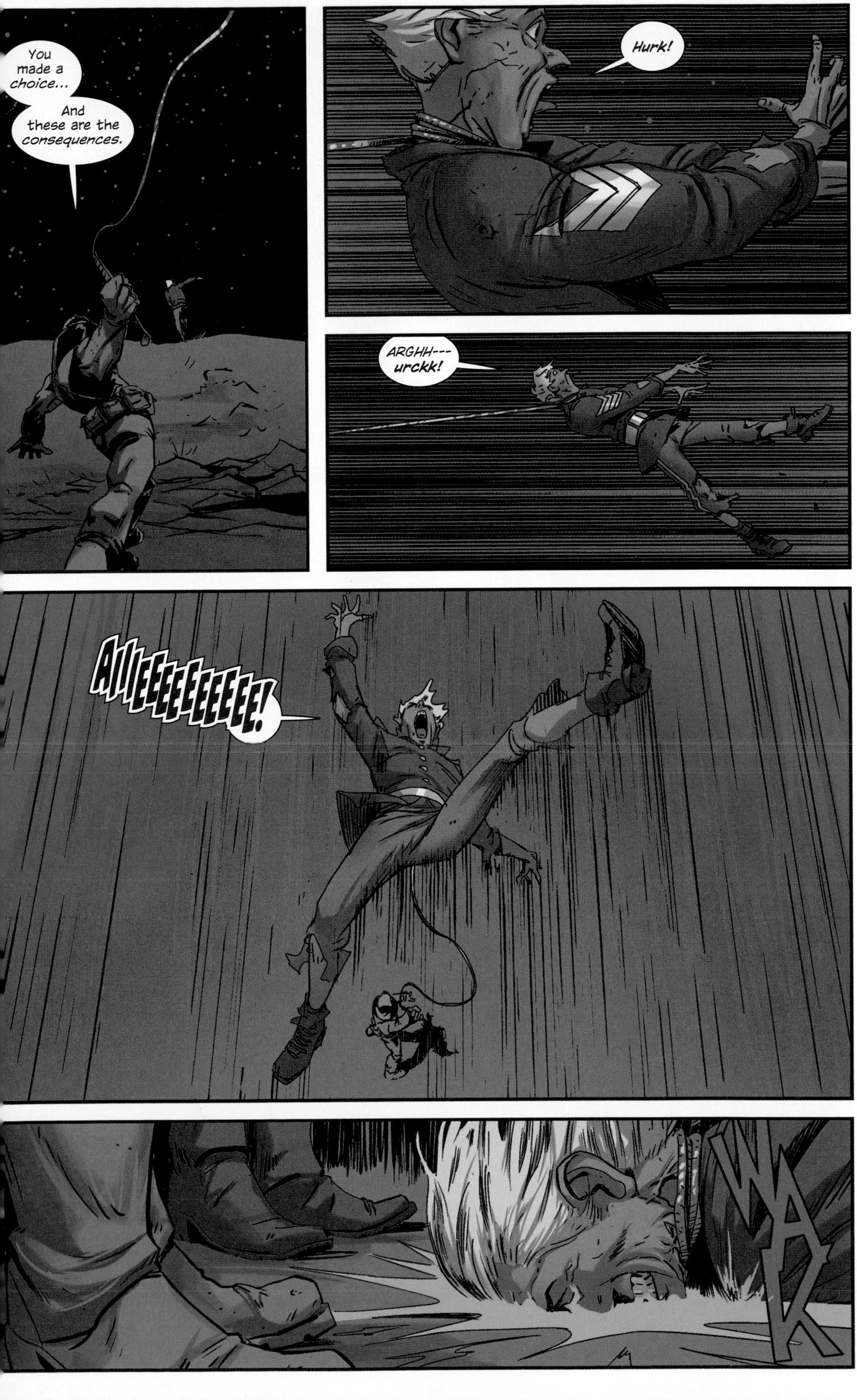
You made a choice...
And these are the consequences.
Hurk!
ARGHH--- urckk!
AIIIEEEEEEEEEE!
WAK

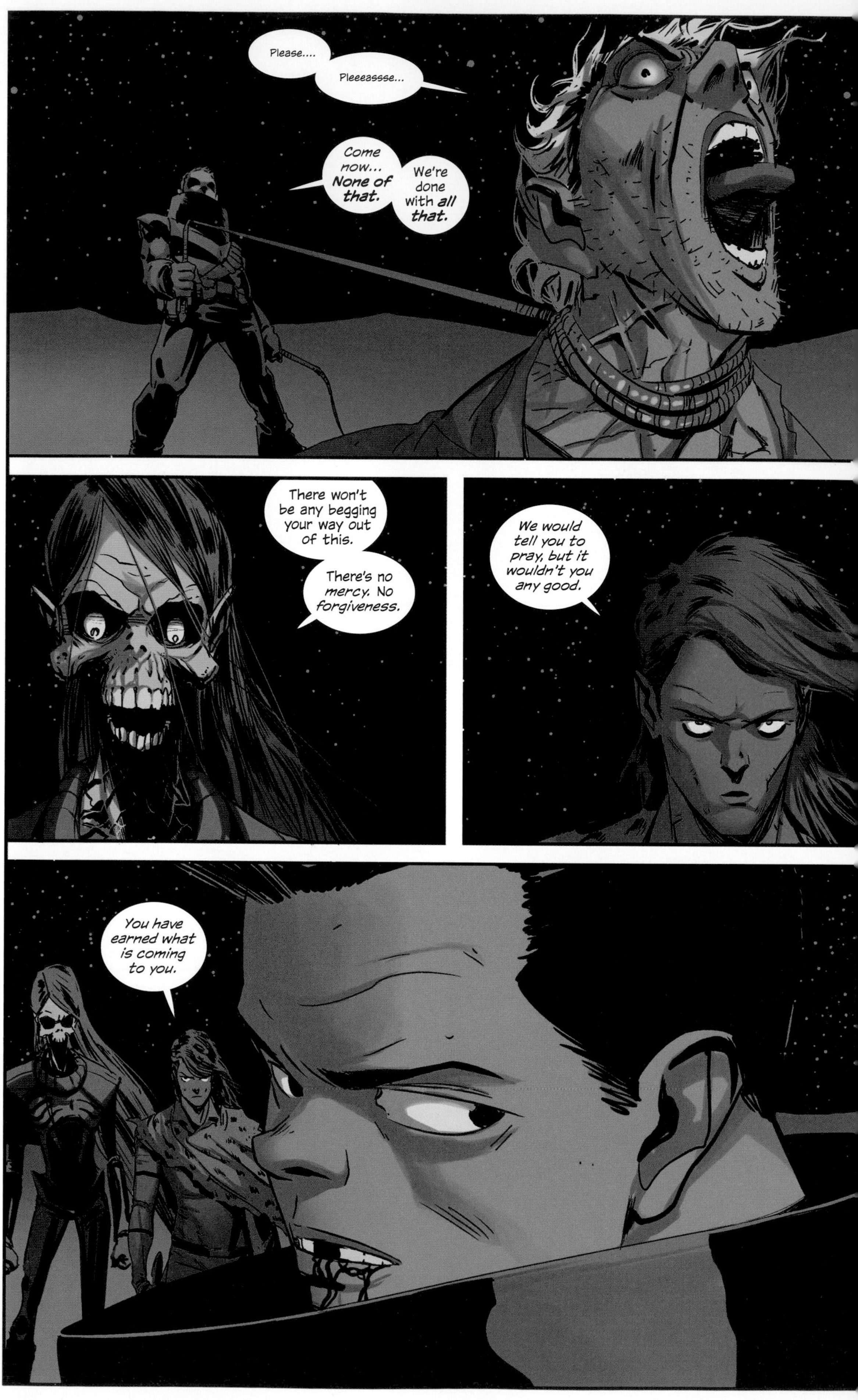
Please....
Pleeeassse...
Come now... None of that.
We're done with all that.
There won't be any begging your way out of this.
There's no mercy. No forgiveness.
We would tell you to pray, but it wouldn't you any good.
You have earned what is coming to you.

HERE'S WHAT I KNOW TO BE
TRUE:

BEFORE IT ALL COMES
CRASHING DOWN, THE PEOPLE
WILL WAKE UP.

IT WILL JUST BE **TOO LATE** TO
DO ANYTHING ABOUT IT.

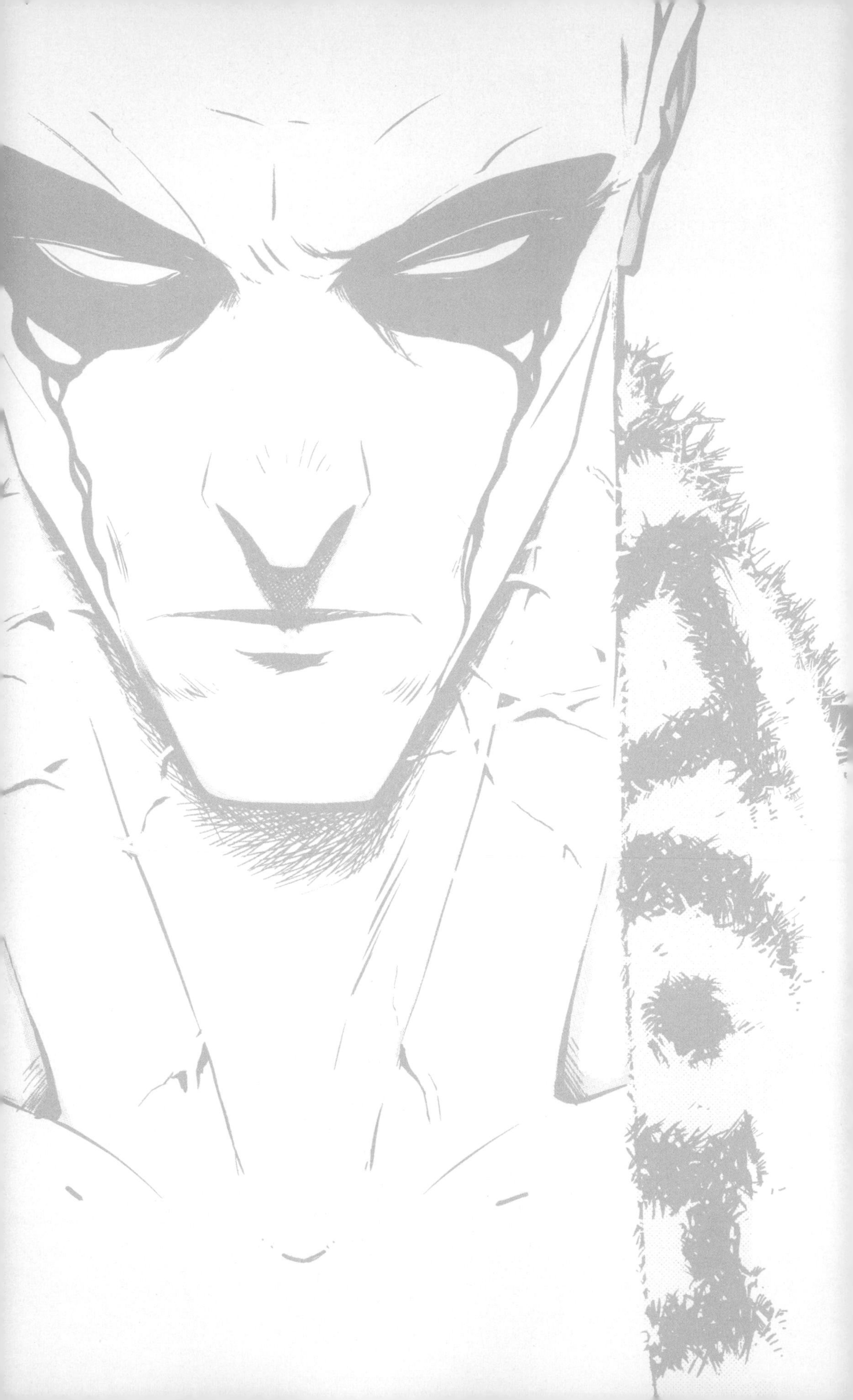

35

THIRTY-FIVE:
TEACH A **MAN** TO **FISH**

I dunno... it's a tough call, Dad.

How you figure that, son?
Askin' a clever boy like yourself in what direction you wanna head shouldn't get you all befuddled. After all, it's only a choice. A preference...
You wanna go left or right?
East or west?
Well...
You're implying that I should just pick one. Randomly. Like it doesn't matter because there's no difference between the two, and, uh...
That's not really how I was raised.
Oink!
Oink!
Exactly! Every decision you make matters. Every single one. It's why Balloon and I ran so many simulations before I made my way into the dangerous and scary outside world.
'Cause bad choices will get you killed every time, and let me tell you, Dad, I've died around one point seven million times...
It is definitely not cool.

What did you just say?

Balloon raised me in a virtual environment. We ran every simulation possible for every potential scenario that I might *have* to face one day.

Sure, there were things we had to skimp on -- like, say, personal preferences, hobbies, snacks -- but we totally had the important things covered. You know, the life and death stuff.

Tell him, Balloon.

...bylon was, and remains now, a ...per-aggressive learner, Horseman.

Like most children, his capacity to consume large quantities of knowledge is rather robust, however your son -- being who and what he is -- has had to subsist on a diet of more serious fare than most his age.

I was programmed to teach him to survive, Death.

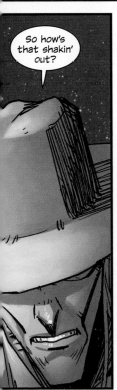

So how's that shakin' out?

Unpredictably. Like now. Factoring out all uncontrollable variables...and factoring in terrain, weather and established danger vectors...

Going east has a sixteen point three percent lower chance of danger. So which way will your son choose?

Well... I'm feeling frisky, Balloon...

I say we go west.

This is easy. Watch.

Pick a flat, smooth stone and then you fling it so...

SPLOOP

SPLOP

TONK

Just get the angle right and let it fly.

Cool.

But I've never done anything like this before.

Okay. Now you try.

Well, son, that's why they call it tryin'.

And just because you haven't done this before doesn't mean you can't, Babylon.

Simply combine two things you have either experienced or studied.

Reference: Precision vectoring and lakeside activities in our database.

All right. Got it. Here goes.

WAK

Well done, young man.

Well done.

So...I respect the work. But how do you get from skippin' rocks to dead fish?

Oh. Well. I combined precision vectoring > target practice with lakeside activities > fishing

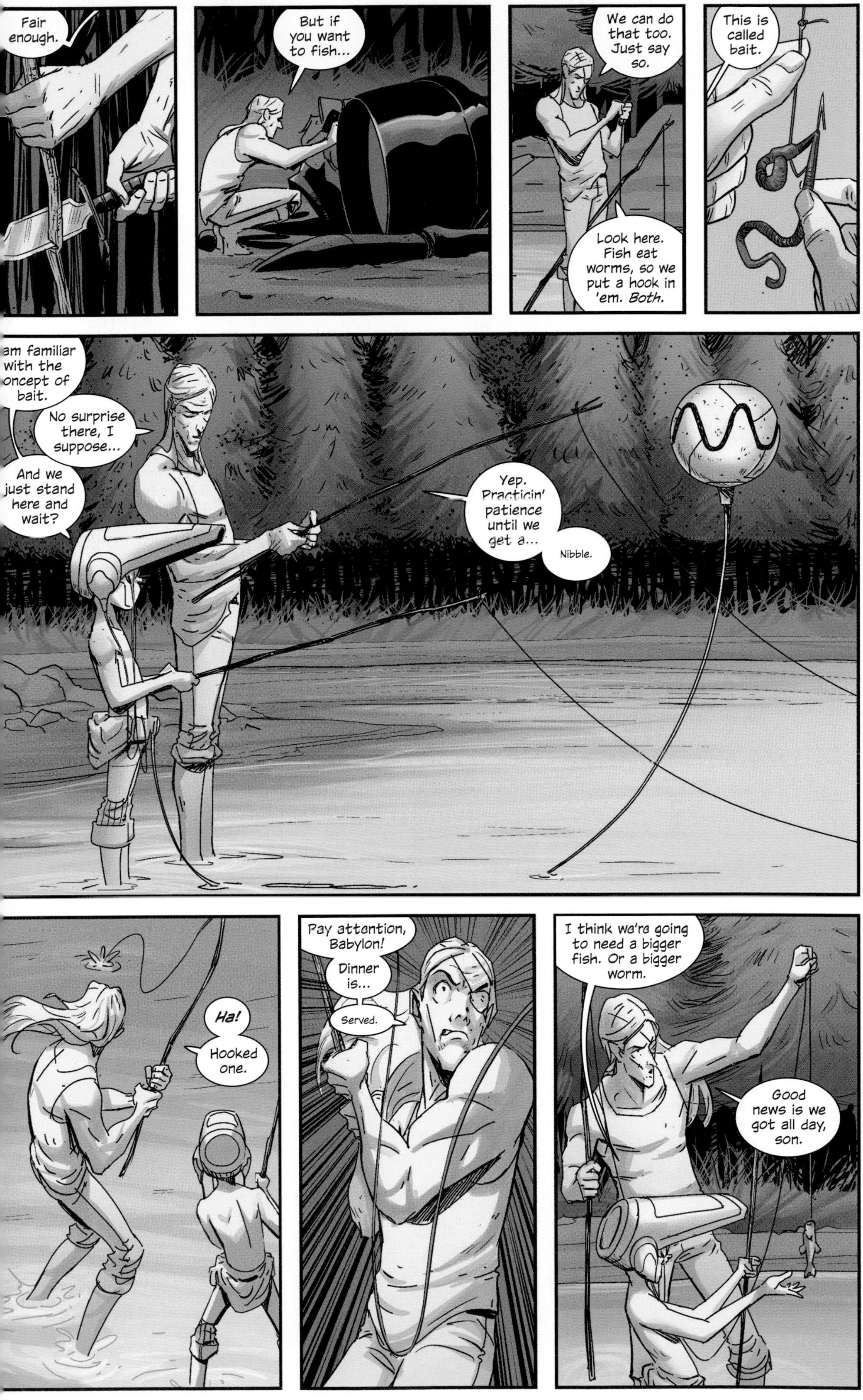
Fair enough.
But if you want to fish...
We can do that too. Just say so.
Look here. Fish eat worms, so we put a hook in 'em. *Both.*
This is called bait.
am familiar with the oncept of bait.
No surprise there, I suppose...
And we just stand here and wait?
Yep. Practicin' patience until we get a...
Nibble.
Ha!
Hooked one.
Pay attention, Babylon!
Dinner is...
Served.
I think we're going to need a bigger fish. Or a bigger worm.
Good news is we got all day, son.

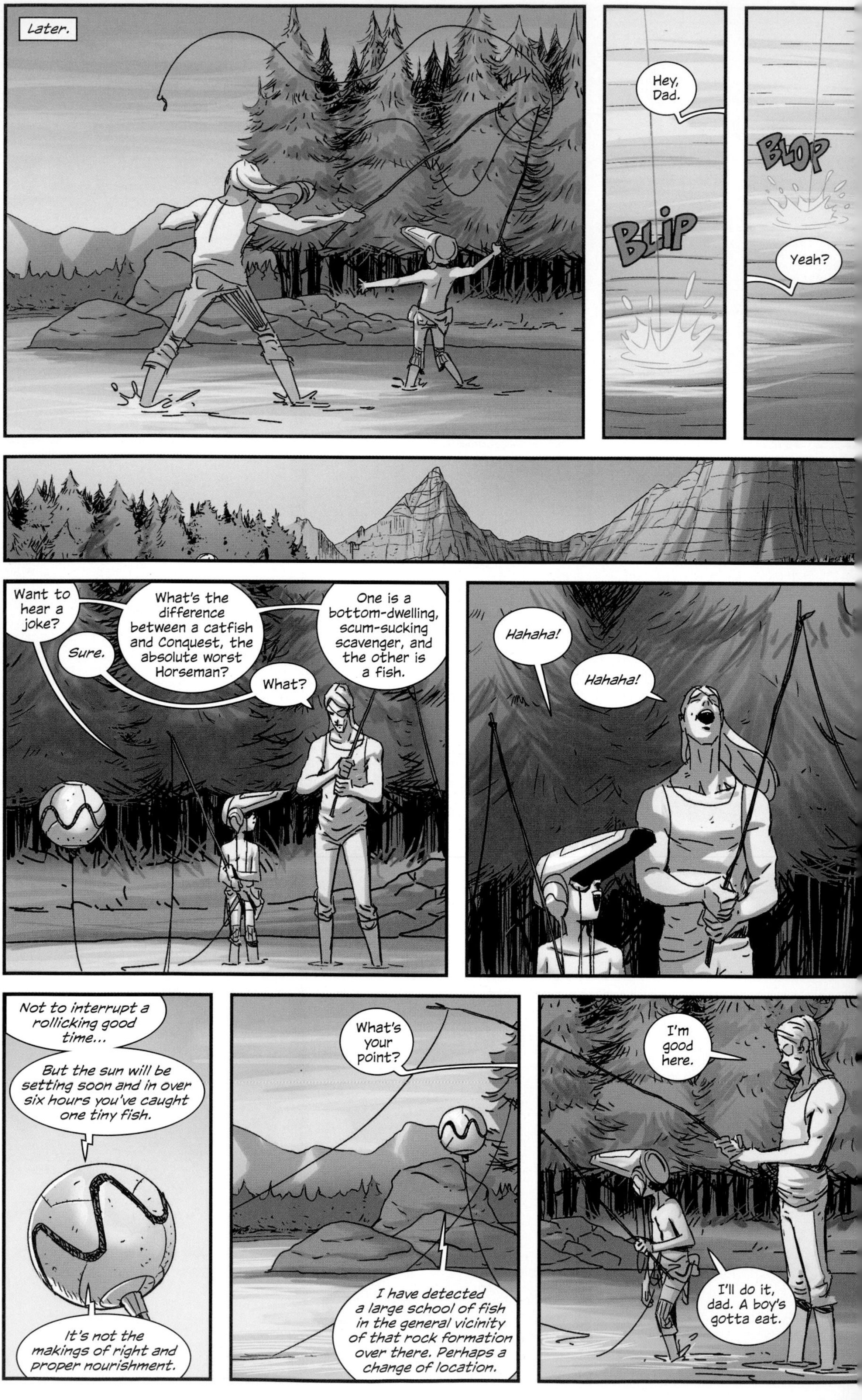

Later.
Hey, Dad.
BLIP
BLOP
Yeah?
Want to hear a joke?
Sure.
What's the difference between a catfish and Conquest, the absolute worst Horseman?
What?
One is a bottom-dwelling, scum-sucking scavenger, and the other is a fish.
Hahaha!
Hahaha!
Not to interrupt a rollicking good time...
But the sun will be setting soon and in over six hours you've caught one tiny fish.
It's not the makings of right and proper nourishment.
What's your point?
I have detected a large school of fish in the general vicinity of that rock formation over there. Perhaps a change of location.
I'm good here.
I'll do it, dad. A boy's gotta eat.

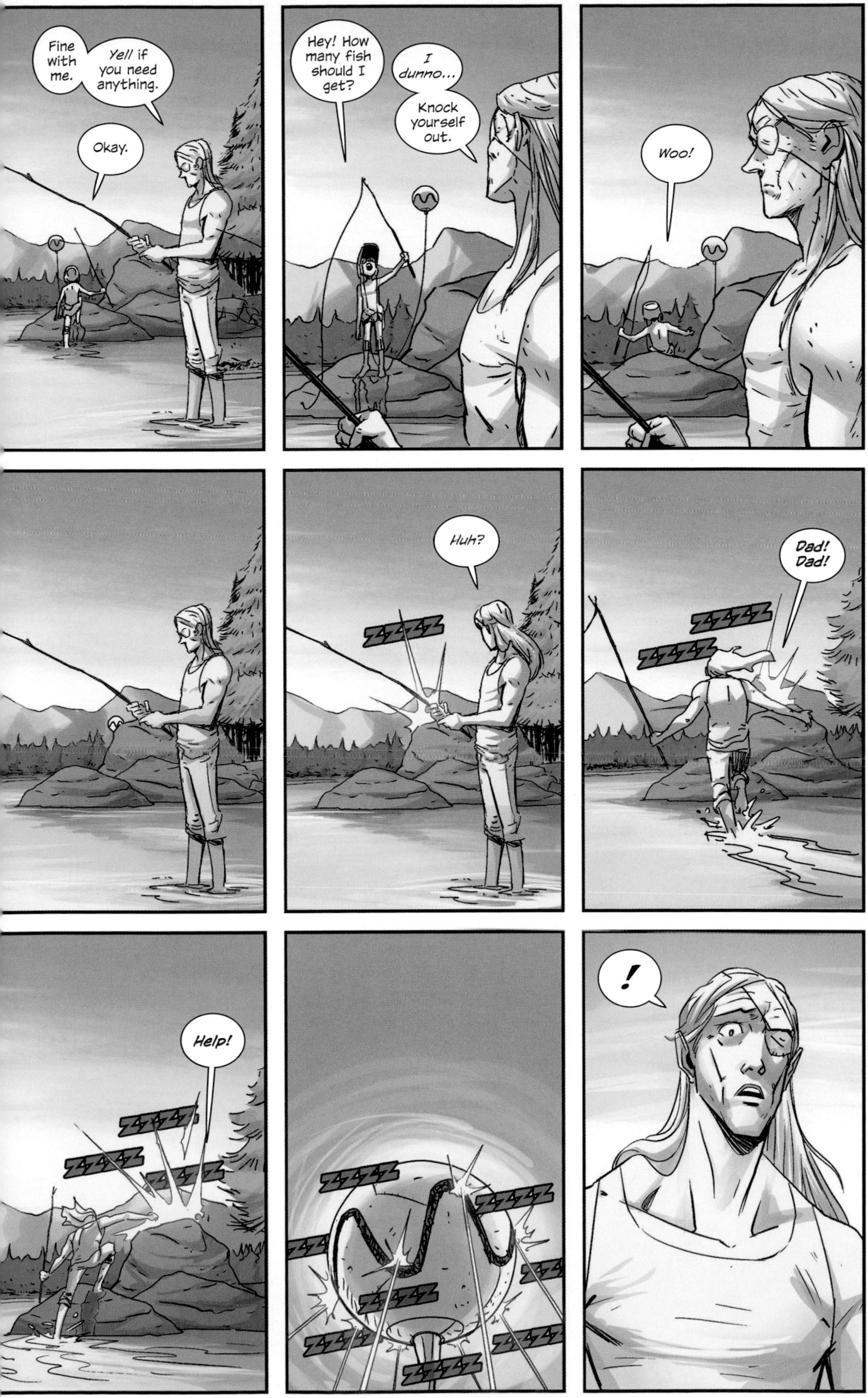
Fine with me.
Yell if you need anything.
Okay.
Hey! How many fish should I get?
I dunno...
Knock yourself out.
Woo!
Huh?
Dad! Dad!
Help!
!

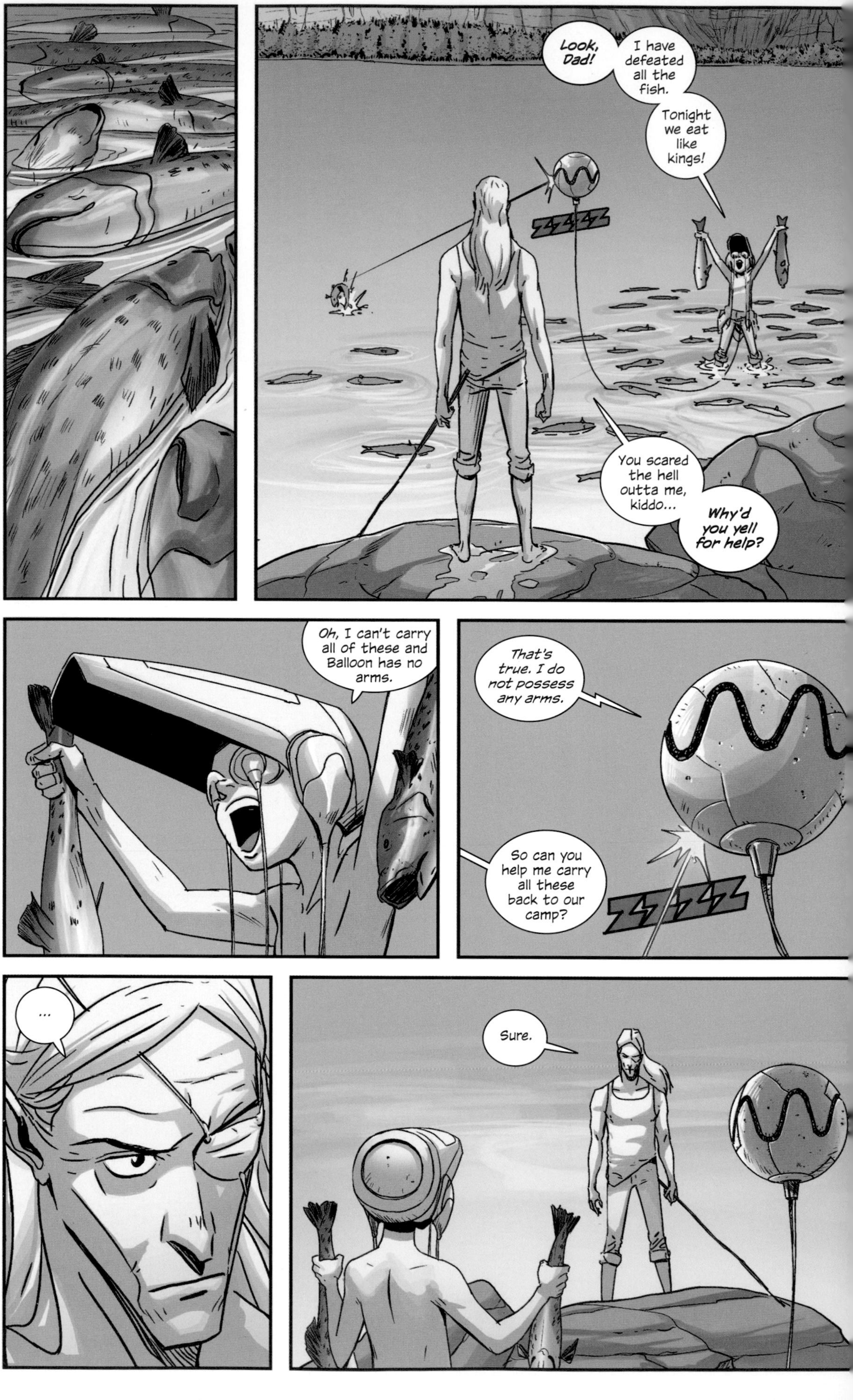

Look, Dad!
I have defeated all the fish.
Tonight we eat like kings!
You scared the hell outta me, kiddo...
Why'd you yell for help?
Oh, I can't carry all of these and Balloon has no arms.
That's true. I do not possess any arms.
So can you help me carry all these back to our camp?
...
Sure.

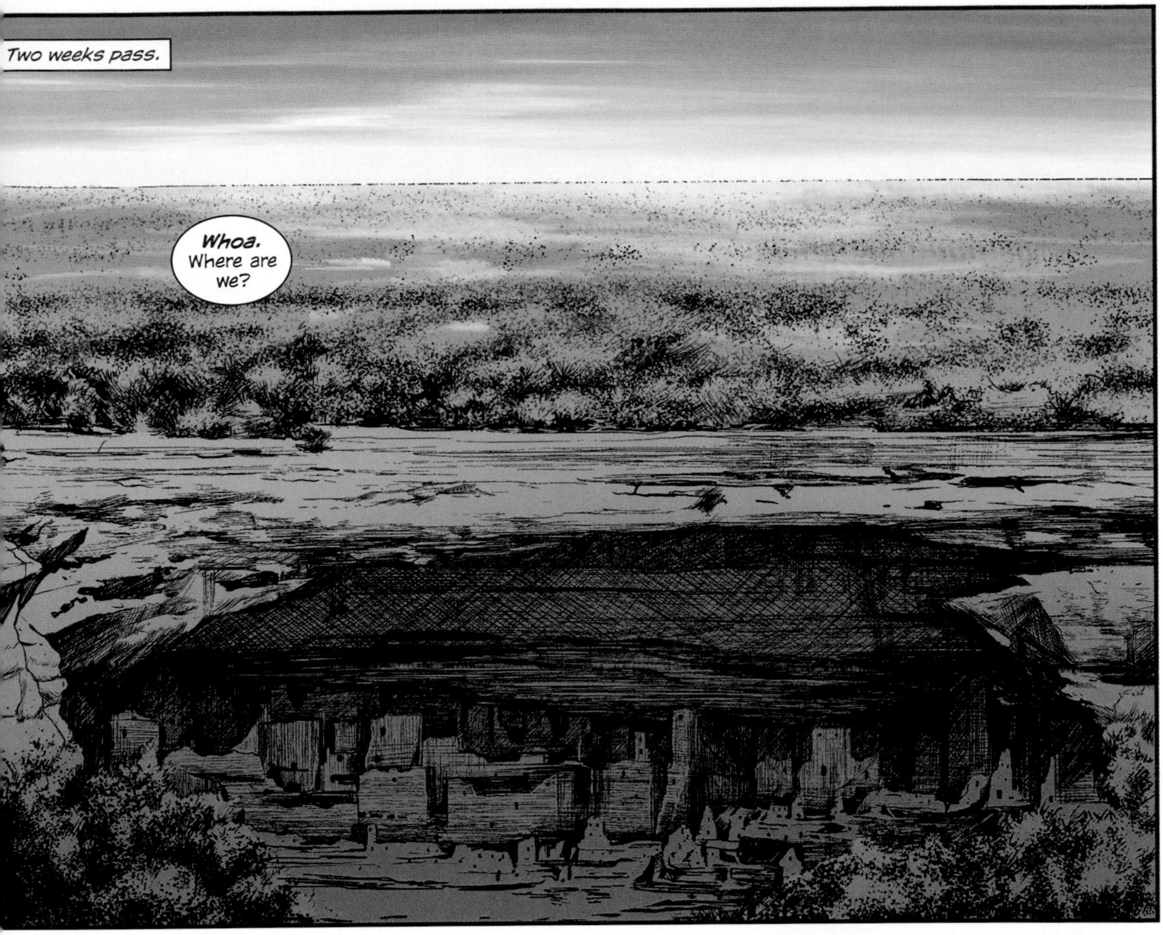
Two weeks pass.
Whoa. Where are we?

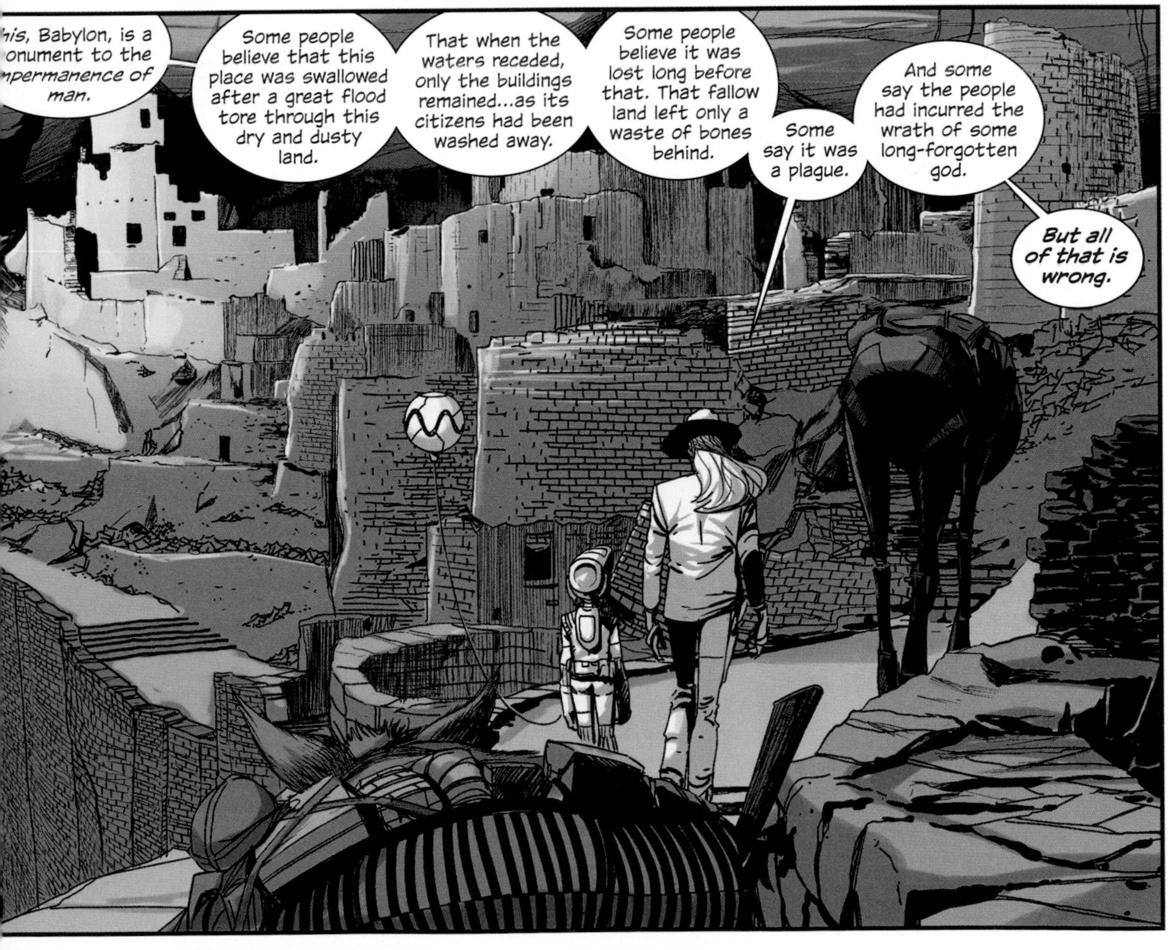
his, Babylon, is a onument to the npermanence of man.
Some people believe that this place was swallowed after a great flood tore through this dry and dusty land.
That when the waters receded, only the buildings remained...as its citizens had been washed away.
Some people believe it was lost long before that. That fallow land left only a waste of bones behind.
Some say it was a plague.
And some say the people had incurred the wrath of some long-forgotten god.
But all of that is wrong.

What happened here was *much* worse.

So I wanted you to see it...

And learn what being *forgotten* looks like.

I dunno, Dad. I think you're overselling it a bit...

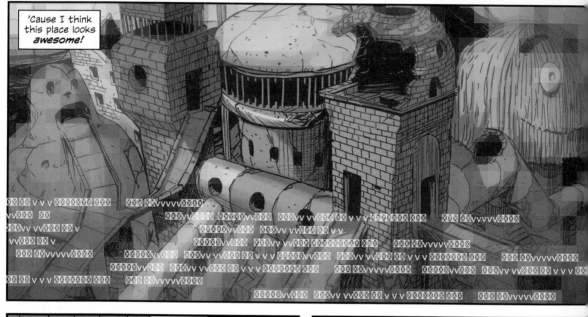

'Cause I think this place looks *awesome!*

I'm going to go see if I can find any cool stuff.

Always looking on the bright side, that one.

Is that how you see it?

Well, I--

Hey, Dad! You're not going to believe what I found...

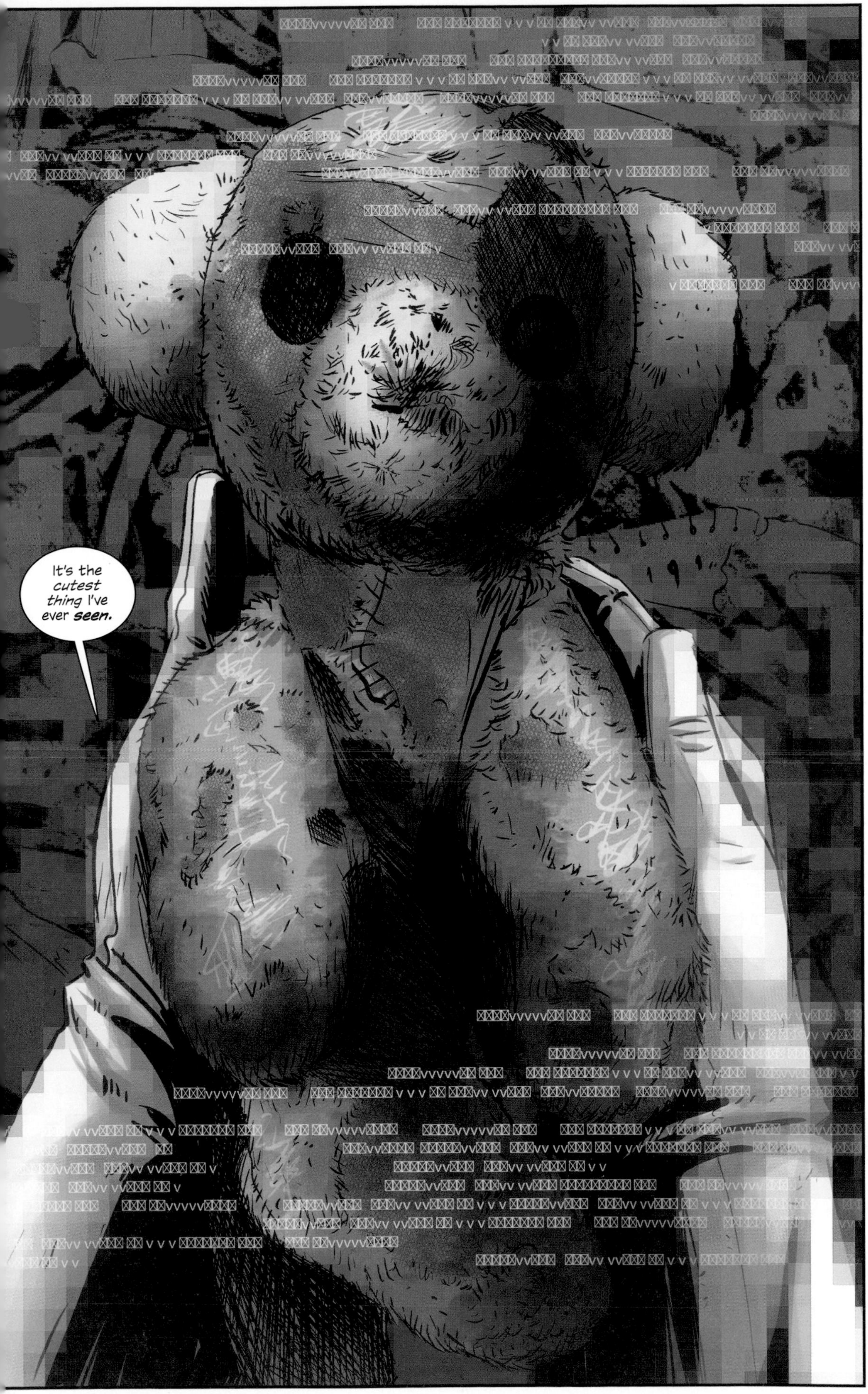
It's the *cutest* *thing* I've ever ***seen.***

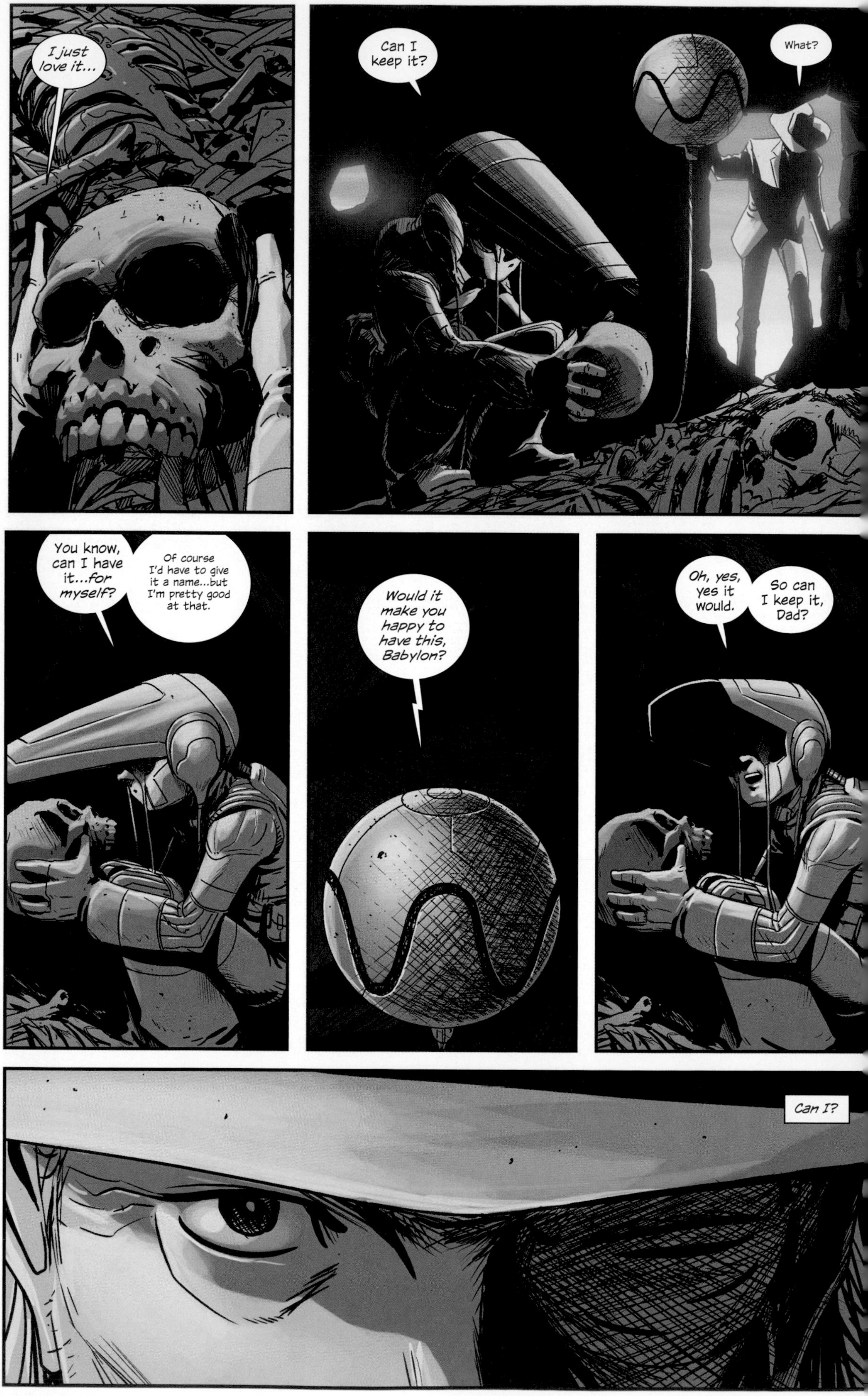
I just love it...
Can I keep it?
What?
You know, can I have it...for myself?
Of course I'd have to give it a name...but I'm pretty good at that.
Would it make you happy to have this, Babylon?
Oh, yes, yes it would.
So can I keep it, Dad?
Can I?

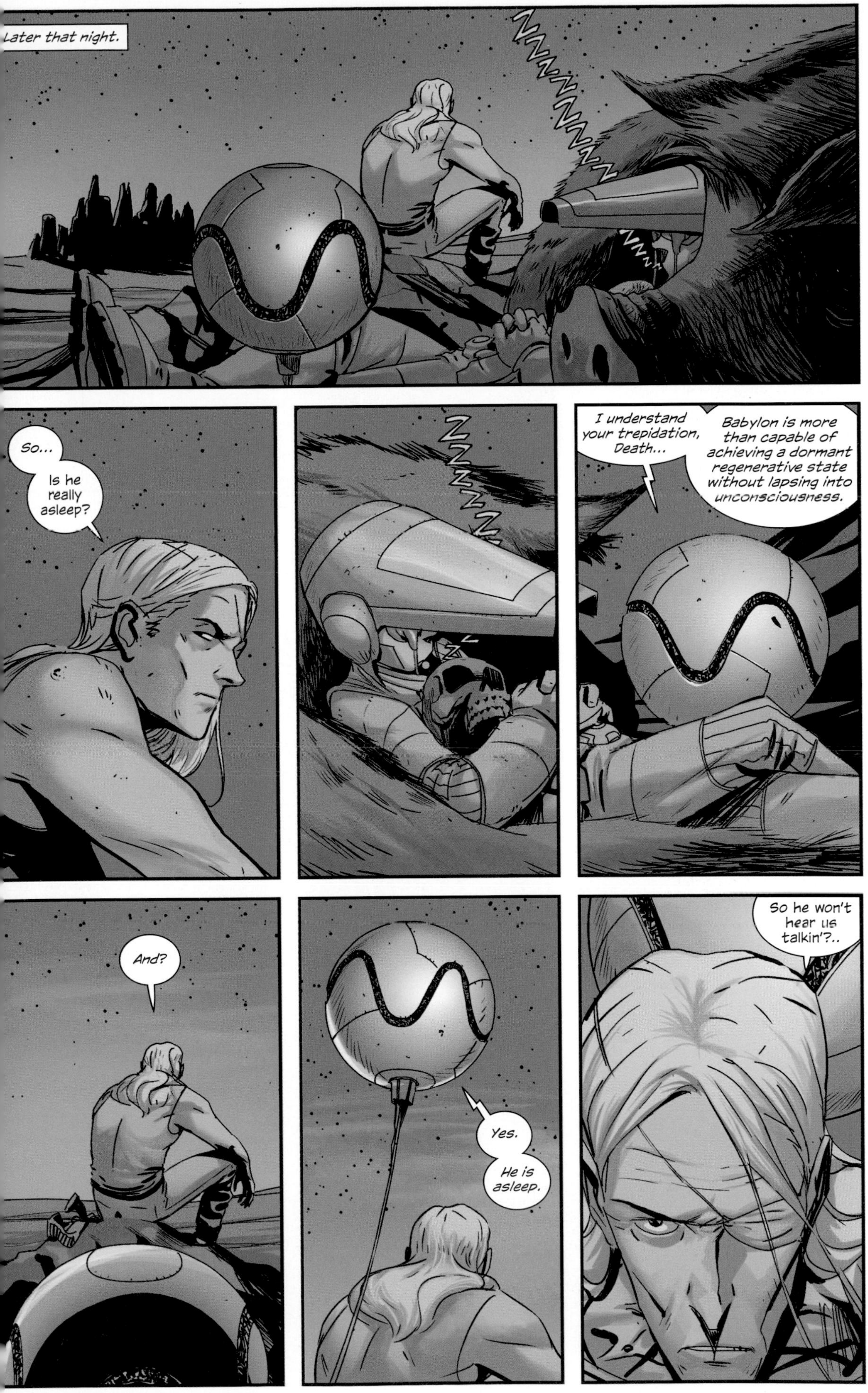
Later that night.
ZZZZZZZZZZ
So...
Is he really asleep?
ZZZZZZ
I understand your trepidation, Death...
Babylon is more than capable of achieving a dormant regenerative state without lapsing into unconsciousness.
And?
Yes.
He is asleep.
So he won't hear us talkin'?..

Not a word that's bein' said?
No. He will not.
Is there something on your mind, Horseman?
Yeah.
What's wrong with him?
I don't understand the question.
The way he reacts to the world around him...
The way he talks about what he sees...
There's somethin' wrong with how his eyes work.

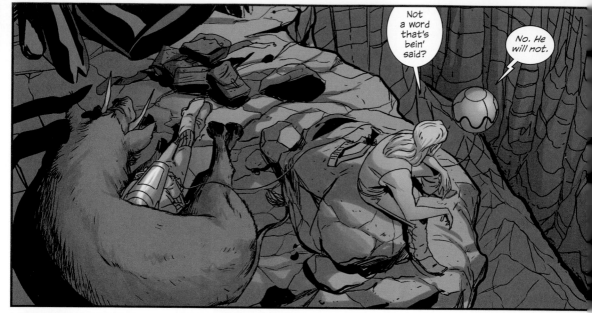

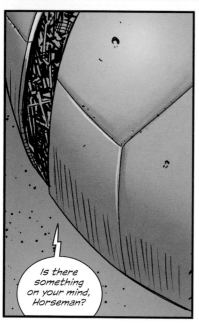

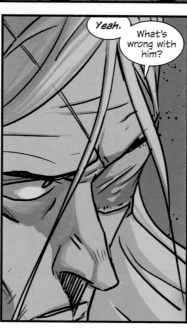

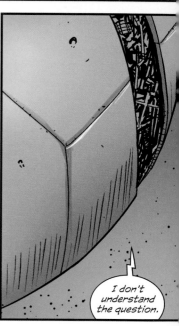

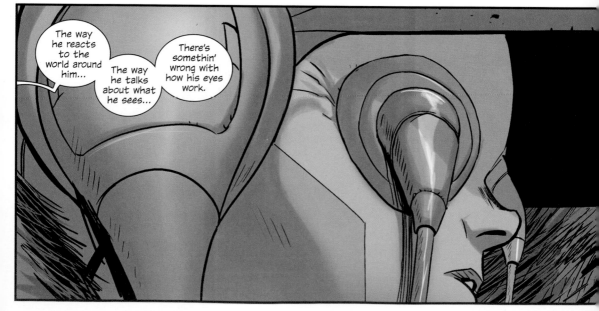

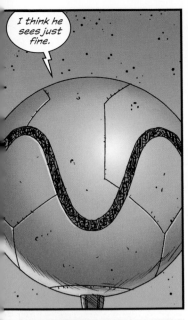

I think he sees just fine.

He don't see the world as it is.

No. He sees something better.

And what's that?

How it should be.

What it can be.

What he can make it.

You need to understand... outside of circumstances like this, there is no division between Babylon and myself.

We are learning how to do... all this together.

We are in unison. Our interests are the same, and we have a higher calling, he and I.

Yeah, well...

Understand this, machine...

Don't fuck it up...

Or you'll be answerin' to a higher power.

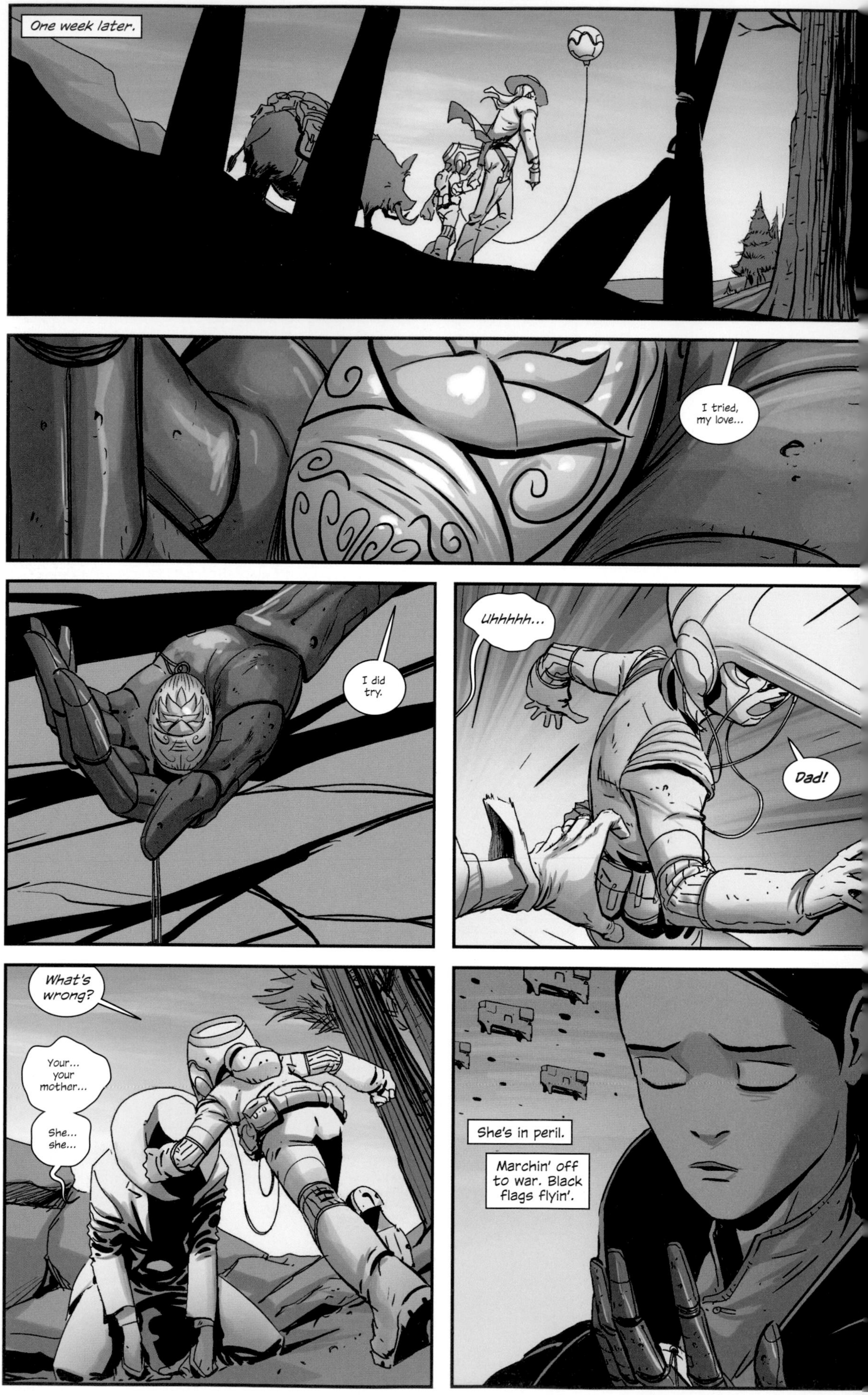
One week later.
I tried, my love...
I did try.
Uhhhhh...
Dad!
What's wrong?
Your... your mother...
She... she...
She's in peril.
Marchin' off to war. Black flags flyin'.

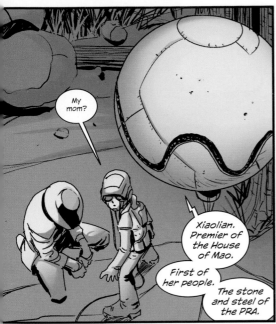

My mom?

Xiaolian. Premier of the House of Mao.

First of her people.

The stone and steel of the PRA.

...

We should help her, Dad.

Don't worry, son...

Nothin' in *this* world...

And nothin' from *any other* could stop me from doin' that.

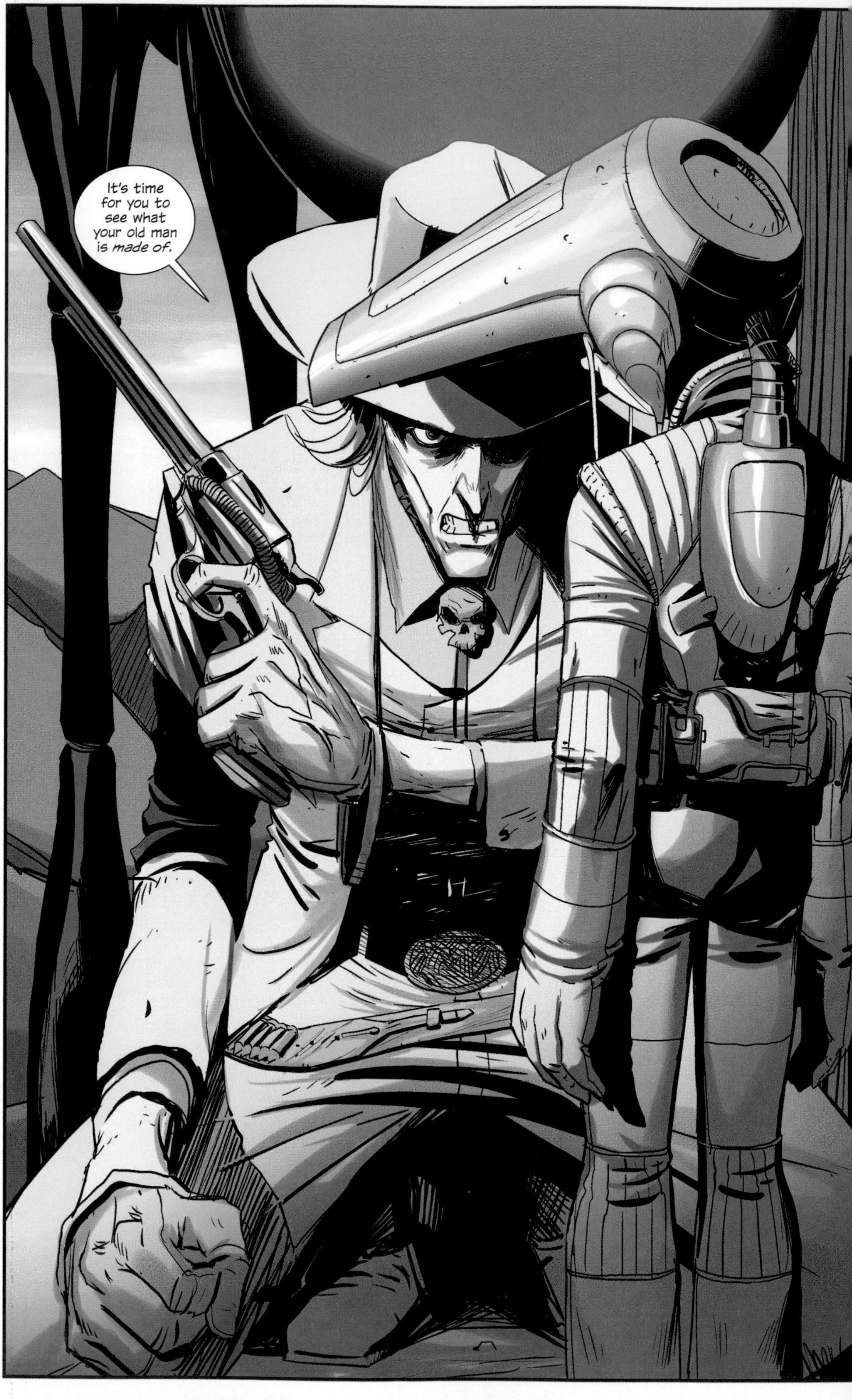
It's time for you to see what your old man is *made of.*

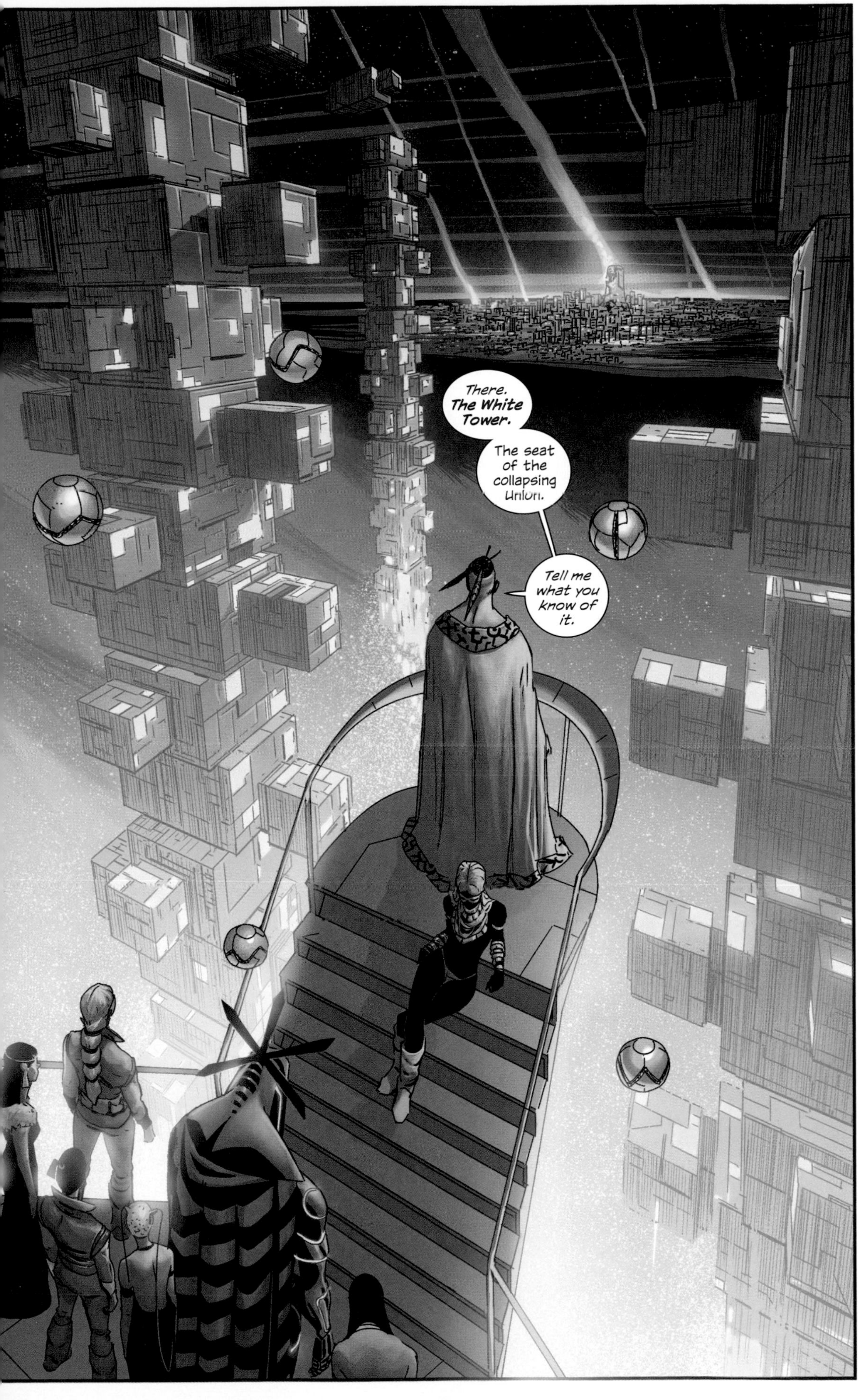
There. **The White Tower.**
The seat of the collapsing Union.
Tell me what you know of it.

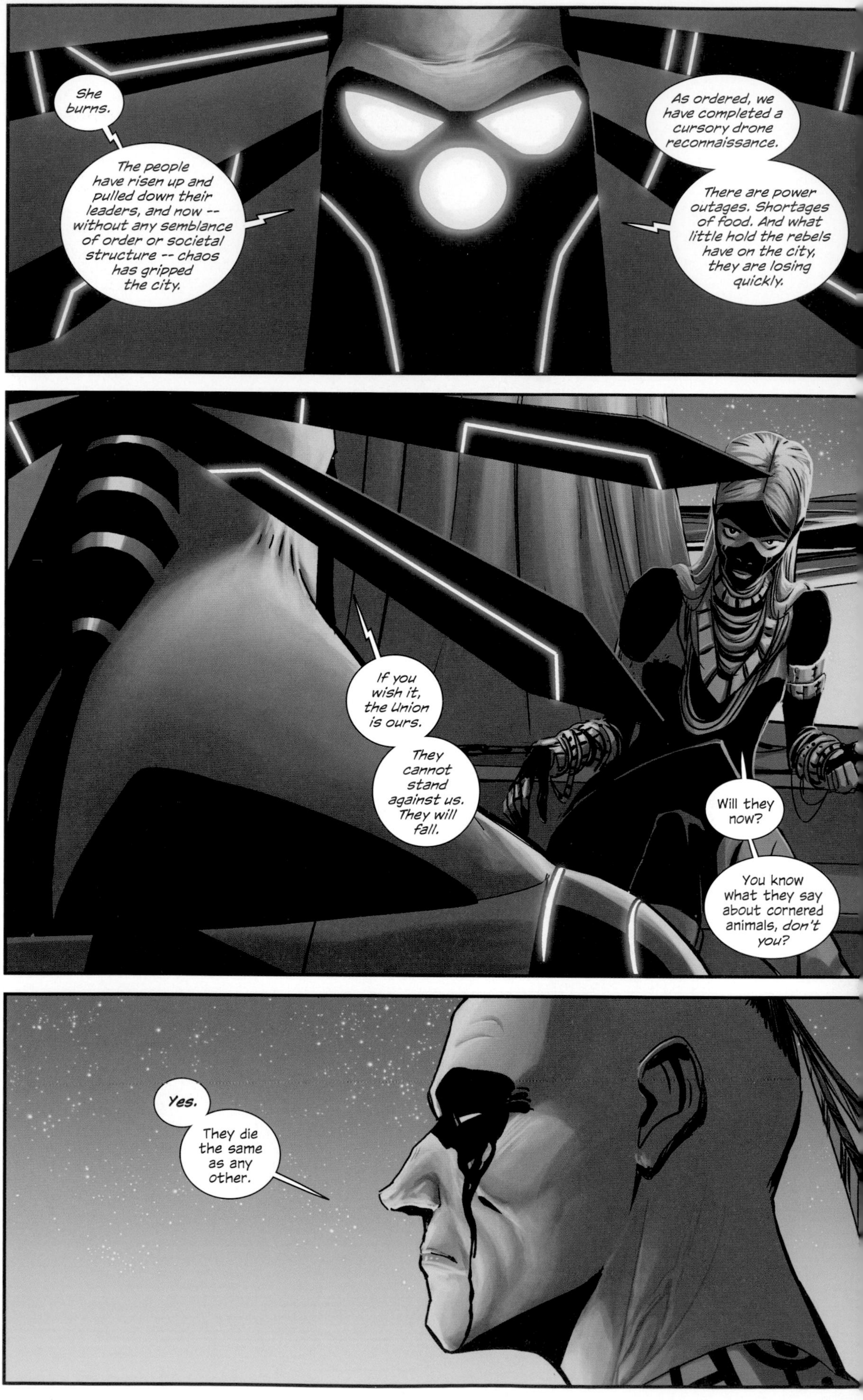
She burns.
The people have risen up and pulled down their leaders, and now -- without any semblance of order or societal structure -- chaos has gripped the city.
As ordered, we have completed a cursory drone reconnaissance.
There are power outages. Shortages of food. And what little hold the rebels have on the city, they are losing quickly.
If you wish it, the Union is ours.
They cannot stand against us. They will fall.
Will they now?
You know what they say about cornered animals, don't you?
Yes.
They die the same as any other.

Chief of Chiefs... you're forgetting something.

It's not surprising, really. Your family has a long history of forgetting *our* ways...

I suppose *your youth* makes you *ignorant* of them as well.

*That place is **bones and bonded**.* Did you even know what that means?

Why don't you tell me, Bodaway?

It means no pureblood member of the Nation can enter the city.

Yes, you could send in your army of Pilgrims...

But I -- or any true son or daughter of the Nation -- would call that victory.

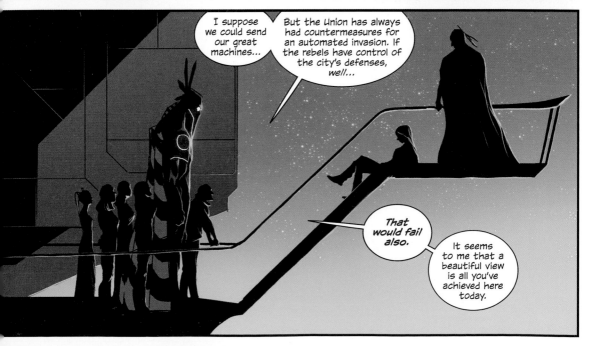

I suppose we could send our great machines...

But the Union has always had countermeasures for an automated invasion. If the rebels have control of the city's defenses, well...

That would fail also.

It seems to me that a beautiful view is all you've achieved here today.

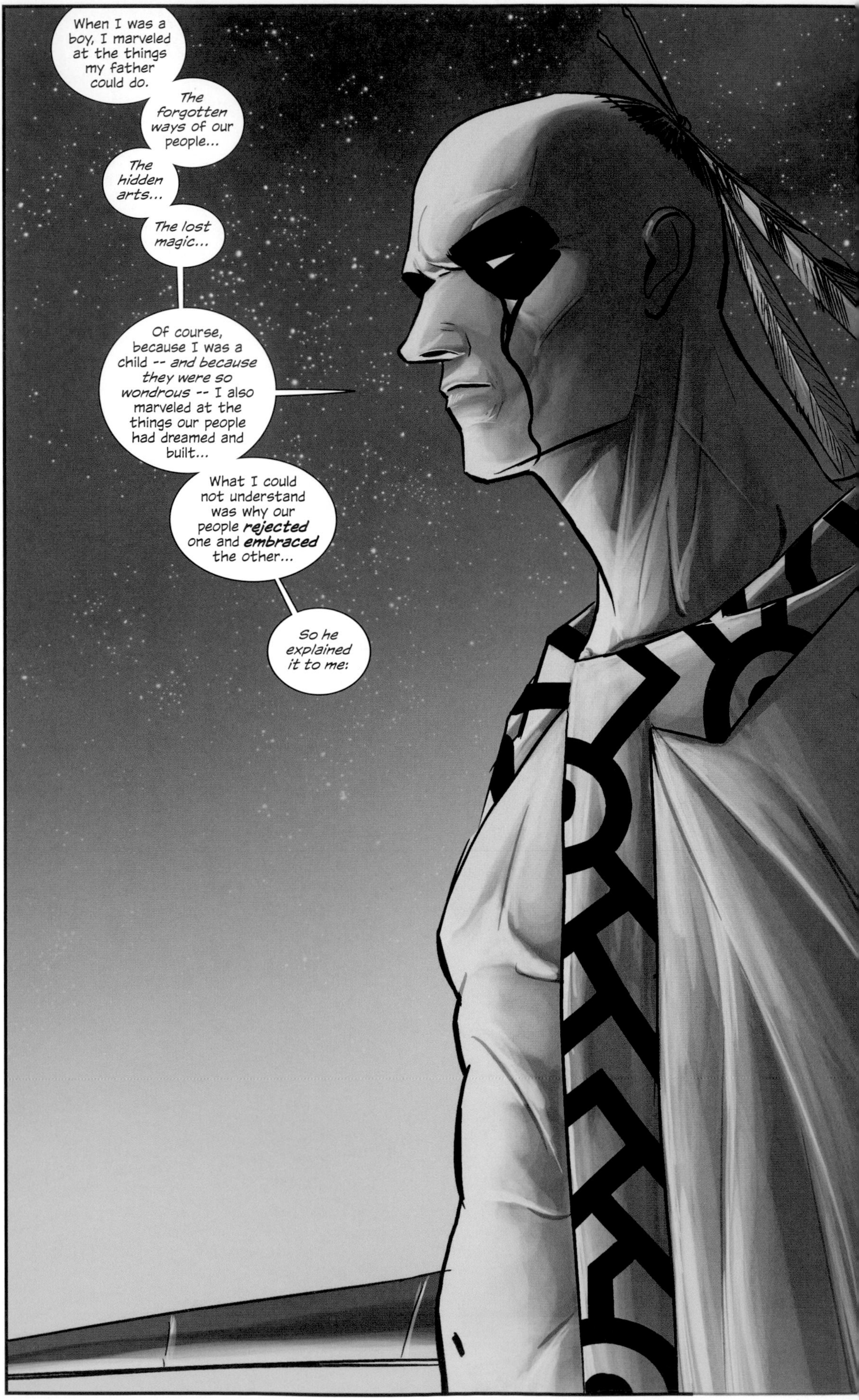
When I was a boy, I marveled at the things my father could do.
The forgotten ways of our people...
The hidden arts...
The lost magic...
Of course, because I was a child -- and because they were so wondrous -- I also marveled at the things our people had dreamed and built...
What I could not understand was why our people rejected one and embraced the other...
So he explained it to me:

"When a conquering nation has no external enemies, it turns its aggression inward."

"A kind of natural schism occurs...and the enemy becomes yourself."

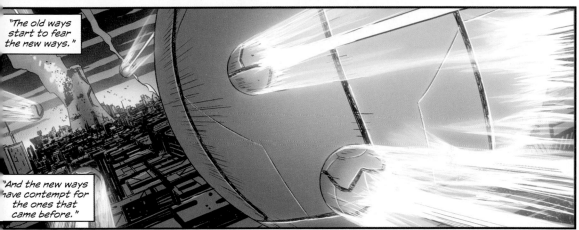

"The old ways start to fear the new ways."

"And the new ways have contempt for the ones that came before."

"The Machine City."

"The Sea of Bones."

BOOM

"Bones and bonded. I know what this means better than you, Bodaway."

"In an foolish effort to recreate the old paradigm of external conflict, the most powerful shaman of their generation came to the Union to do big magic."

"They would make the capital unwelcome to our kind, so that the Union could flourish unfettered."

"And they succeeded."

"They died closing the loop of their spell, and now just look at all the enemies we have gathered unto ourselves the last century."

"Just look at how we have withered under the weight of all our progress."

"I am bringing our lost brothers and sisters home."

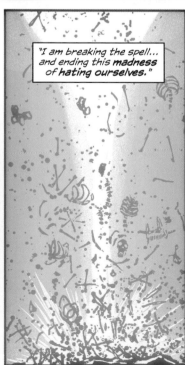

"I am breaking the spell... and ending this **madness** of **hating ourselves.**"

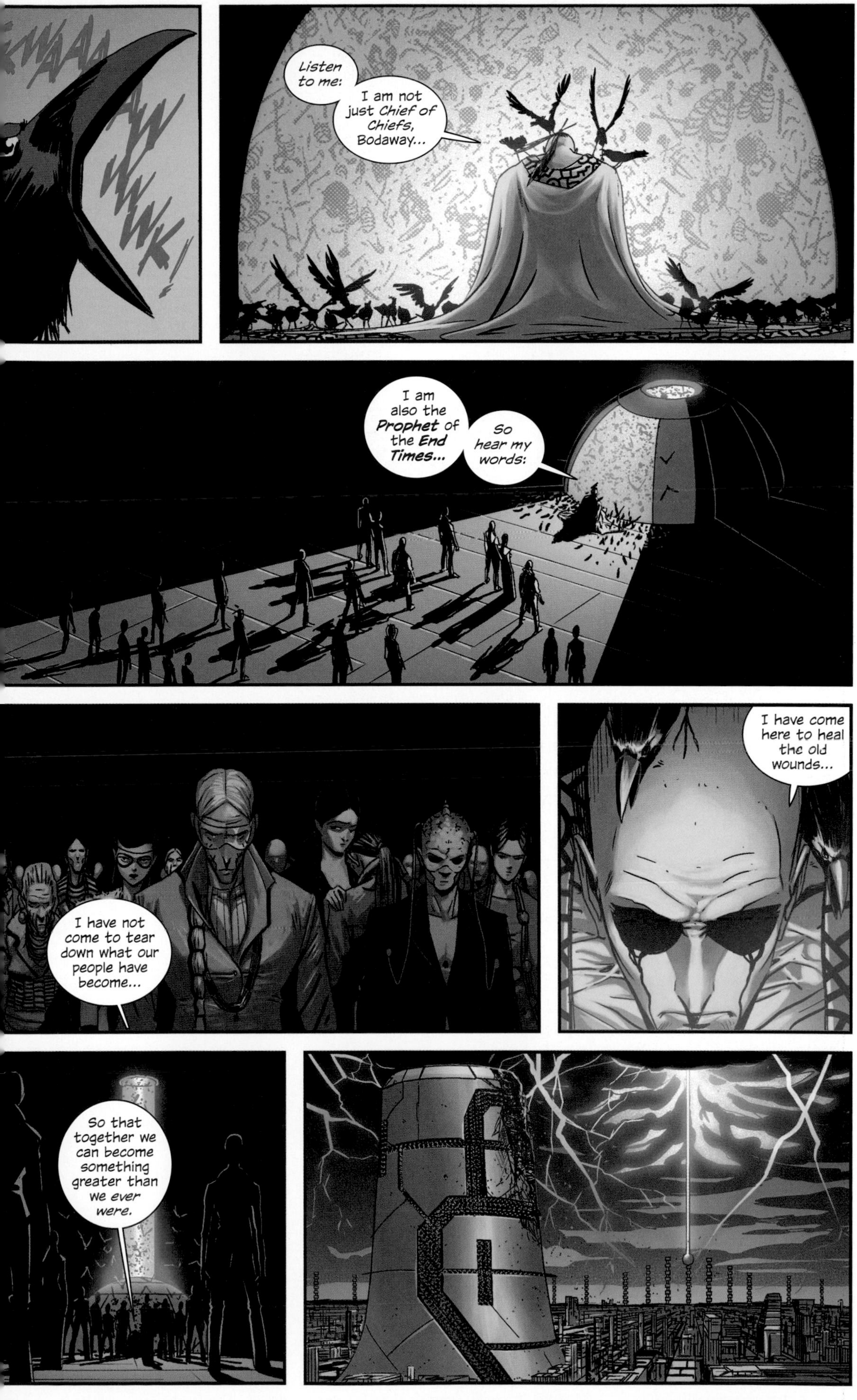

Listen to me:
I am not just *Chief of Chiefs*, Bodaway...
I am also the ***Prophet*** of the ***End Times...***
So hear my words:
I have not come to tear down what our people have become...
I have come here to heal the old wounds...
So that together we can become something greater than we *ever* were.

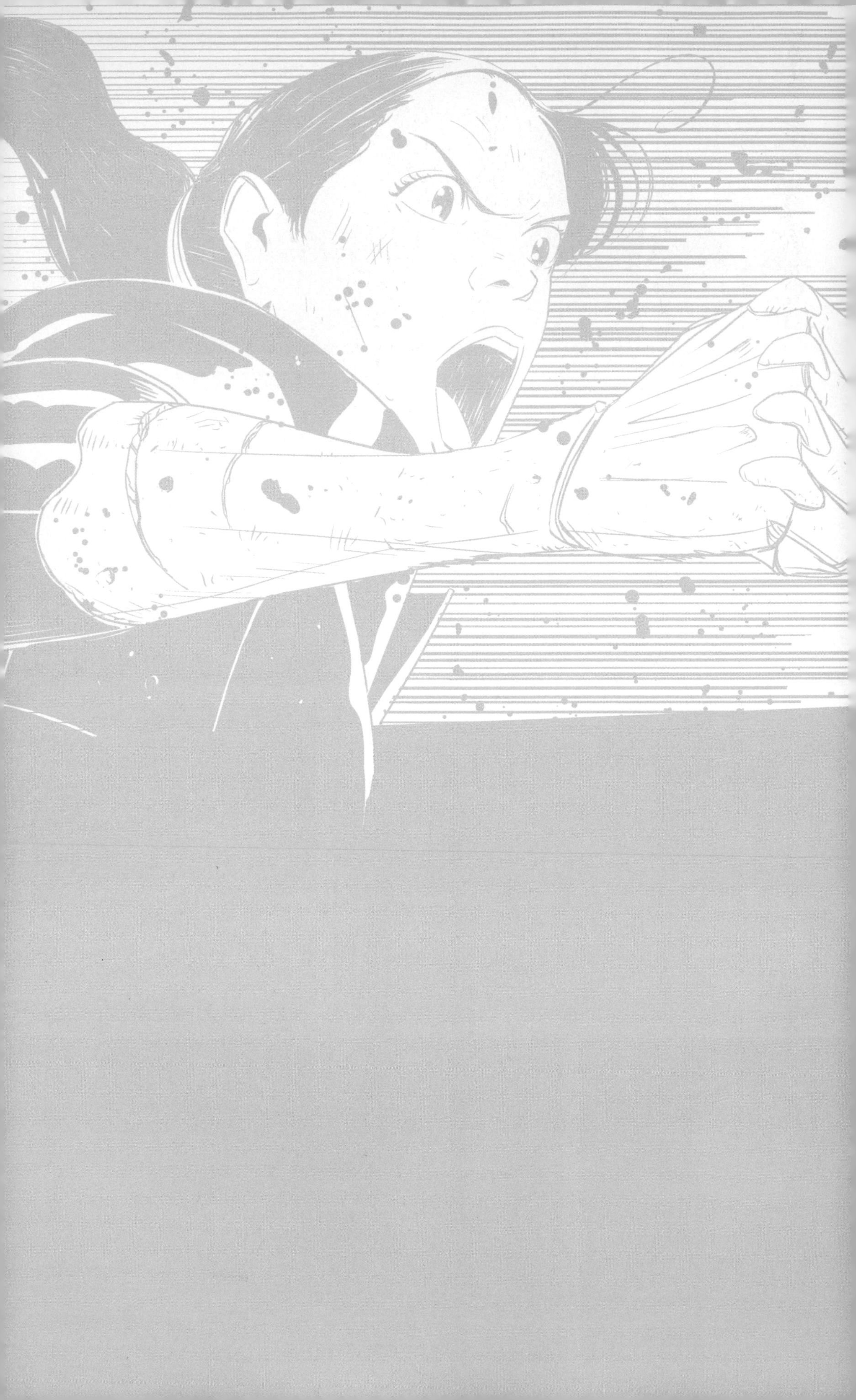

36

THIRTY-SIX:
THIS IS **REAL**
REVOLUTION

YOUR **END** WILL BE THE
SAME AS **THEIRS.**

THERE IS **NOTHING**
SPECIAL ABOUT **YOU.**

no days later.

We have gained control of the power grid, the automated city functions, and suppressed what little resistance remained following the recent uprising...

"The population is subdued."

"Establishing a perimeter now."

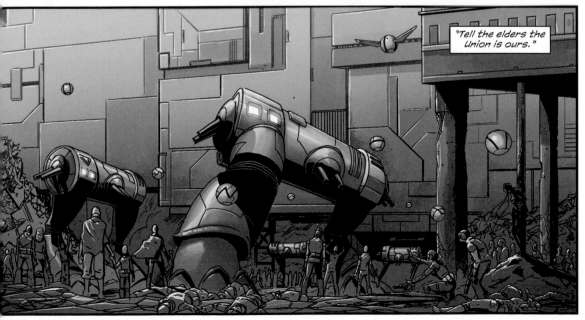

"Tell the elders the Union is ours."

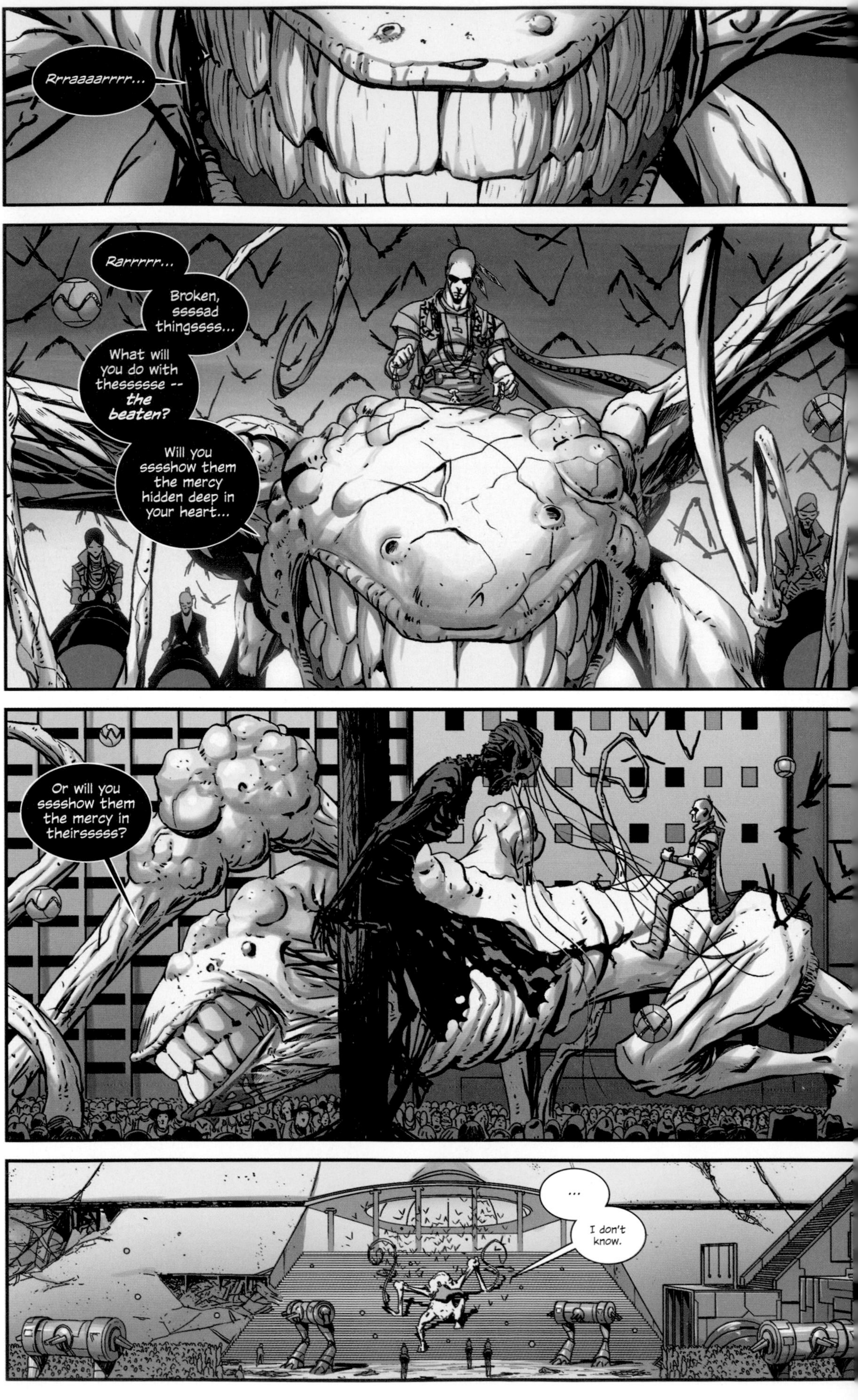
Rrraaaarrrr...
Rarrrrr...
Broken, ssssad thingssss...
What will you do with thesssse -- *the beaten?*
Will you ssshow them the mercy hidden deep in your heart...
Or will you sssshow them the mercy in theirsssss?
...
I don't know.

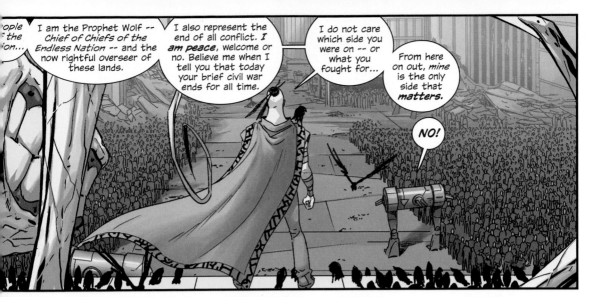

I am the Prophet Wolf -- Chief of Chiefs of the Endless Nation -- and the now rightful overseer of these lands.

I also represent the end of all conflict. **I am peace**, welcome or no. Believe me when I tell you that today your brief civil war ends for all time.

I do not care which side you were on -- or what you fought for...

From here on out, *mine* is the only side that *matters*.

NO!

No! This is shit! Total shit!

You will be silent, citizen.

Fuck off! I will be *heard!*

This is wrong! All wrong!

What were you expecting, child?

Tell me... I will listen.

We fought against *corruption* and oppression...

We fought to free ourselves from those who saw us as inferior -- *subhuman*. They... they treated us like animals...

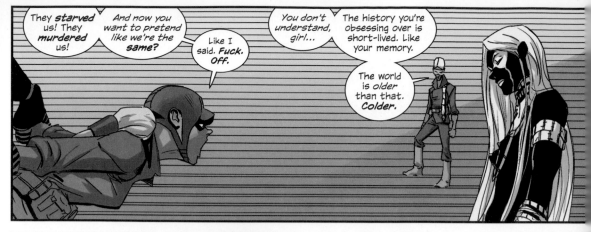

They **starved** us! They **murdered** us!

And now you want to pretend like we're the **same**?

Like I said. **Fuck. Off.**

You don't understand, girl!...

The history you're obsessing over is short-lived. Like your memory.

The world is *older* than that. *Colder.*

Perhaps we should round all of you up -- *warriors or not* -- and march you north in blankets of affliction.

Either you all choose mercy, or the Nation shows you how long all our memories are.

I know which I would prefer...

What of you, Chief of Chiefs?

My words were clear...

Peace for *all.*

It's wrong. *It's wrong!*

I...

I...

It wasn't supposed to be this way.

We..we won.

These are end times, child...

There are no righteous left among the living.

And what you're feeling...that's the hopelessness of a conquered people.

*Fight it... don't fight it...*We leave it to you.

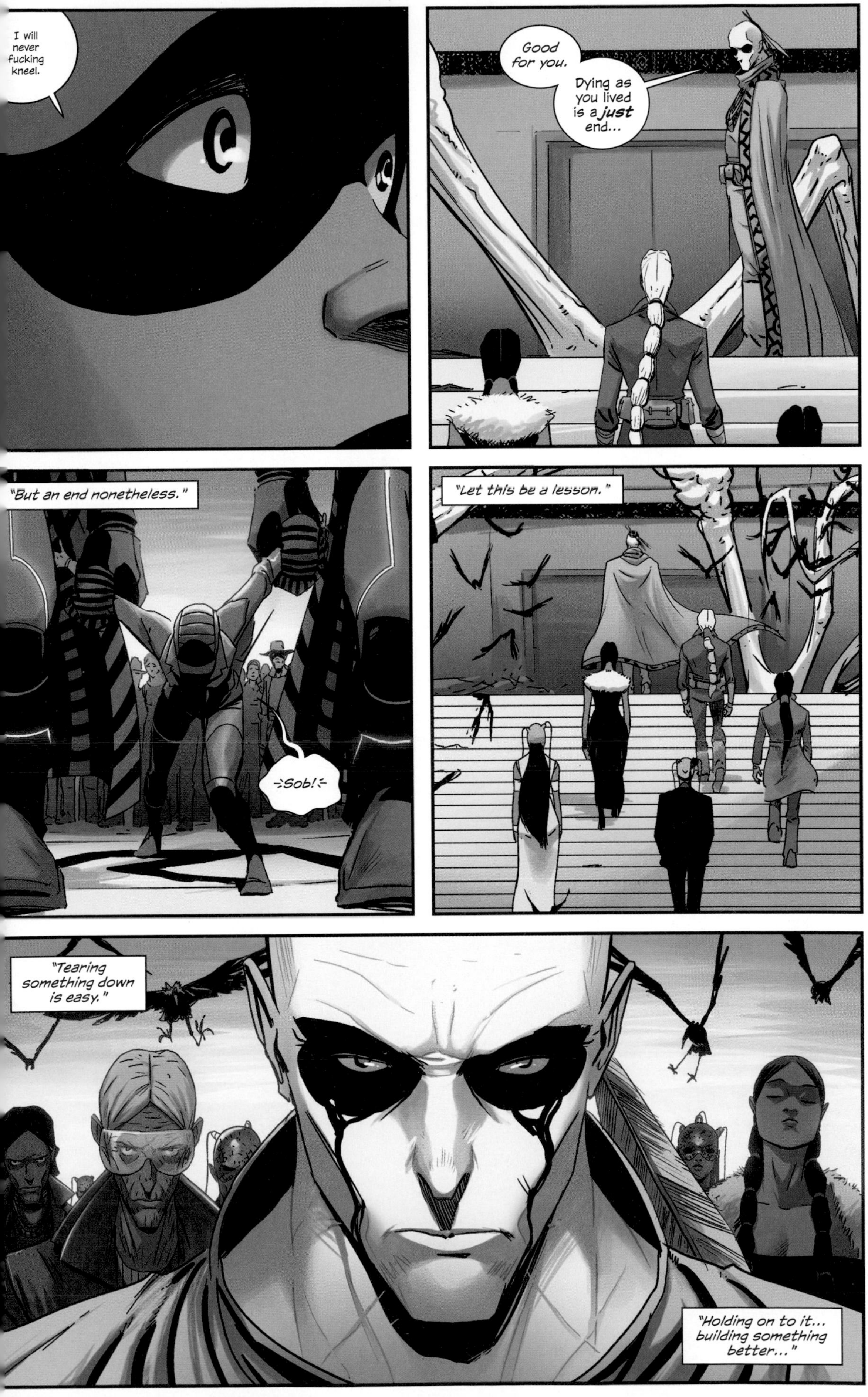
I will never fucking kneel.
Good for you.
Dying as you lived is a **just** end...
"But an end nonetheless."
-Sob!-
"Let this be a lesson."
"Tearing something down is easy."
"Holding on to it... building something better..."

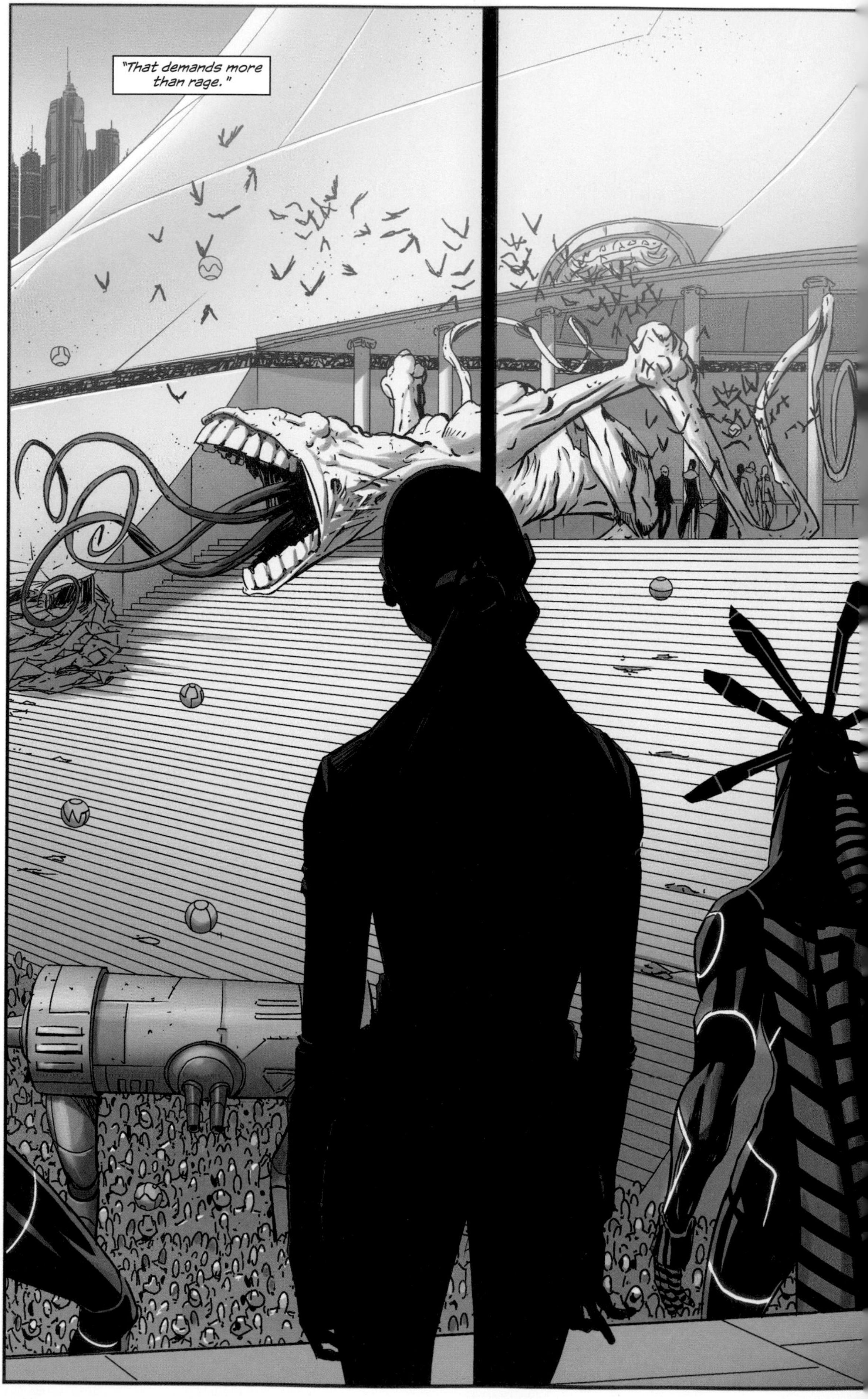
"That demands more than rage."

WE HAVE **TAKEN** ALL
THAT YOU **HAVE.**

WE WILL **ERASE** ALL
THAT YOU **WERE.**

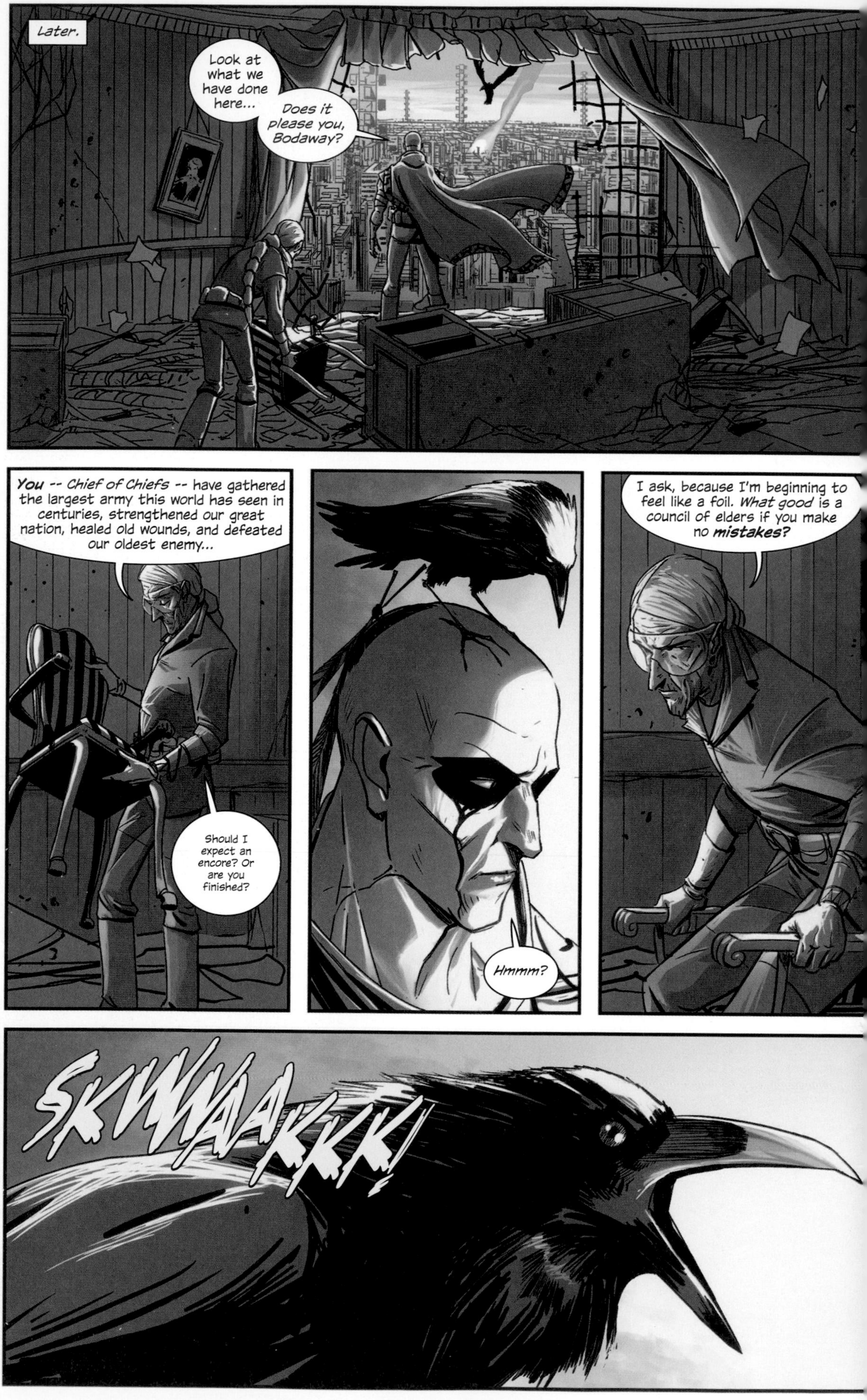
Later.
Look at what we have done here...
Does it please you, Bodaway?
You -- Chief of Chiefs -- have gathered the largest army this world has seen in centuries, strengthened our great nation, healed old wounds, and defeated our oldest enemy...
Should I expect an encore? Or are you finished?
Hmmm?
I ask, because I'm beginning to feel like a foil. What good is a council of elders if you make no mistakes?
SKWAAKKK!

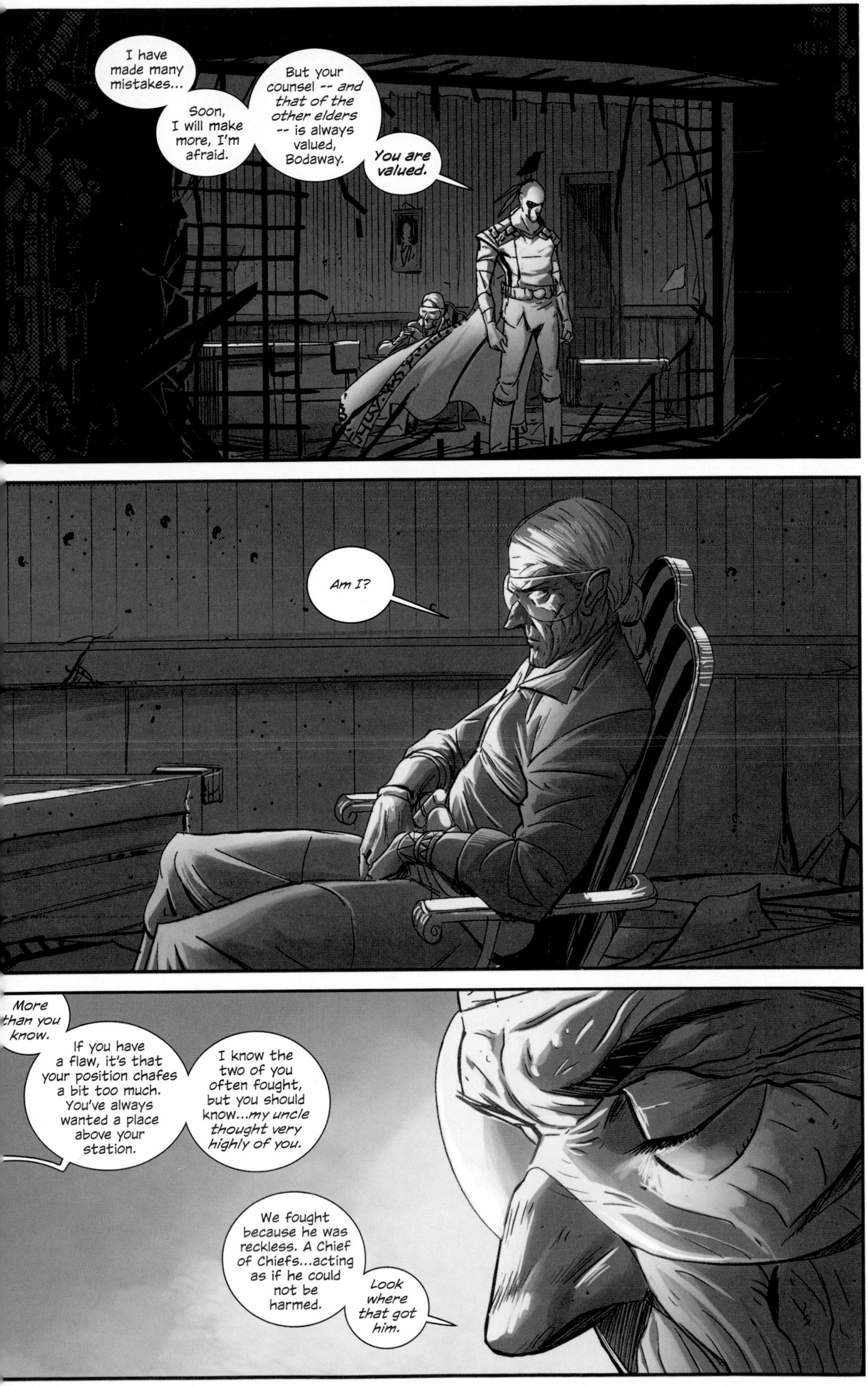
I have made many mistakes...
Soon, I will make more, I'm afraid.
But your counsel -- and that of the other elders -- is always valued, Bodaway.
You are valued.
Am I?
More than you know.
If you have a flaw, it's that your position chafes a bit too much. You've always wanted a place above your station.
I know the two of you often fought, but you should know...my uncle thought very highly of you.
We fought because he was reckless. A Chief of Chiefs...acting as if he could not be harmed.
Look where that got him.

He was 'reckless' because he knew he had the elders -- *you* -- to take his place if needed.

In that spirit, I am leaving the Union in your hands.

Ha!

Mind telling me why?

Because my role here is done...

But the Prophet's?

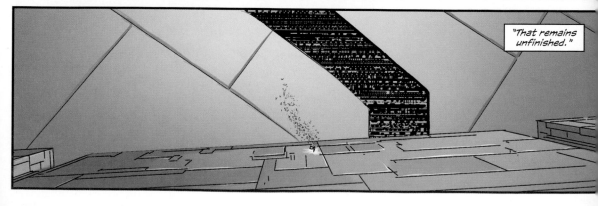

"That remains unfinished."

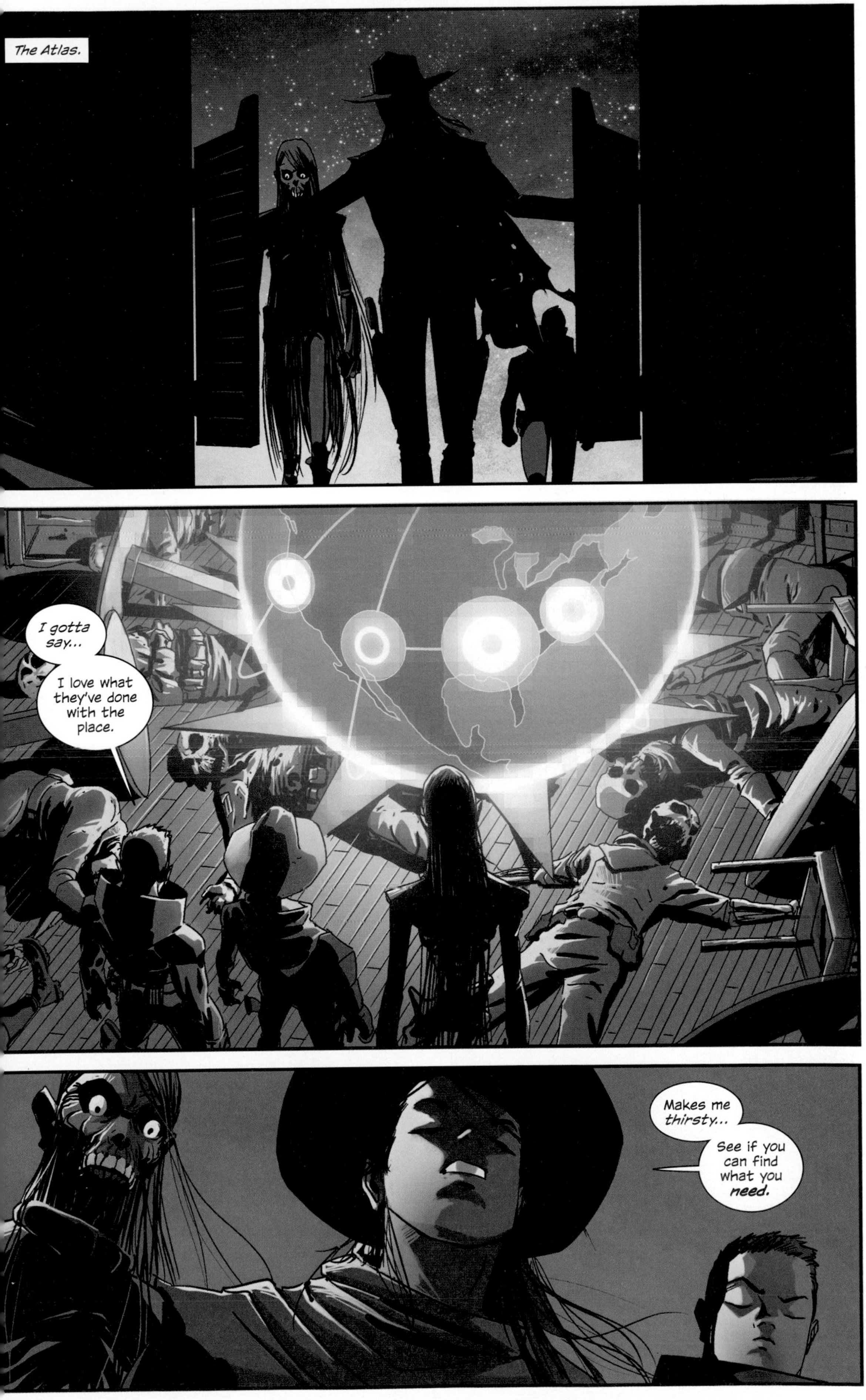
The Atlas.
I gotta say...
I love what they've done with the place.
Makes me thirsty...
See if you can find what you need.

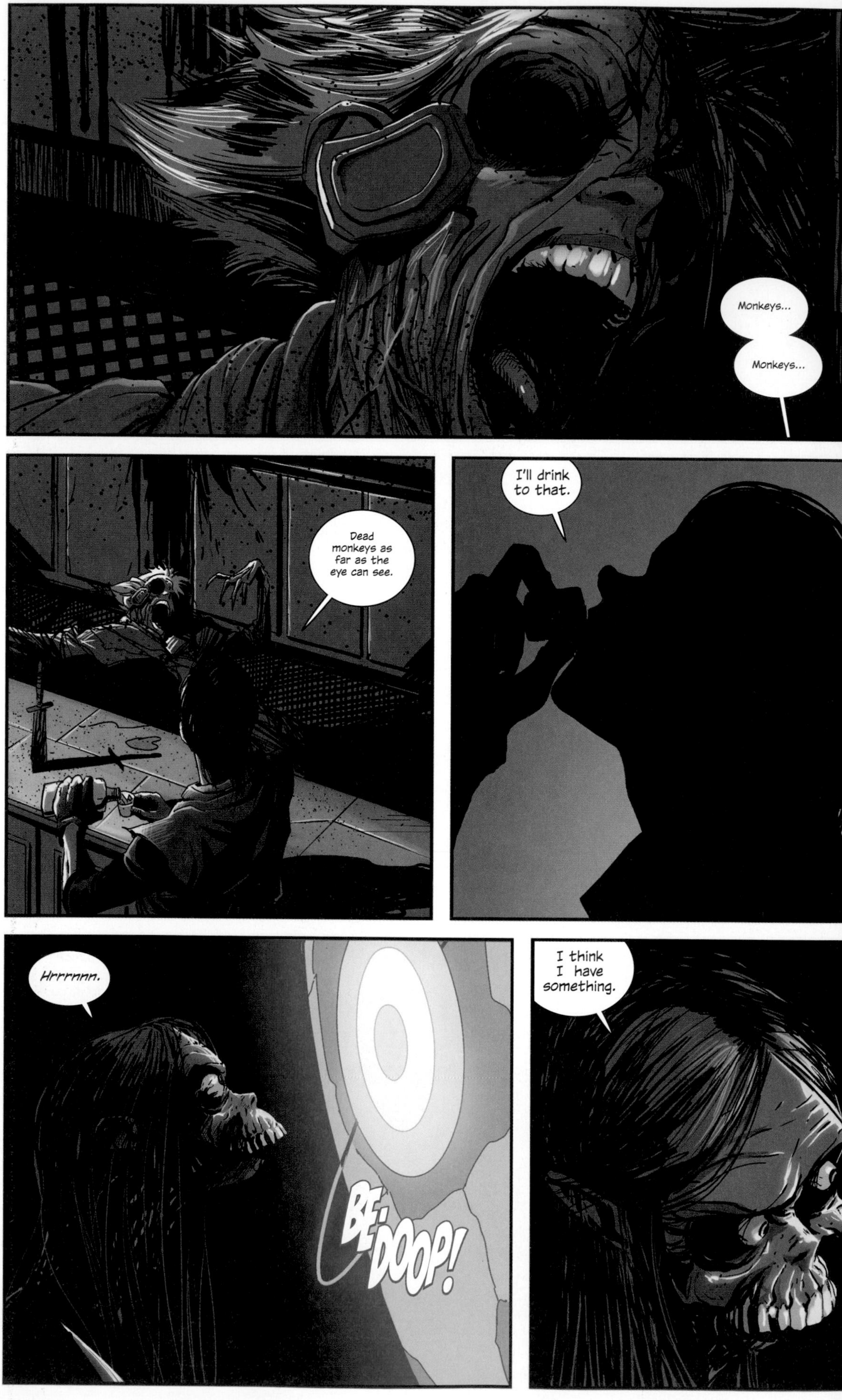
Monkeys...
Monkeys...
Dead monkeys as far as the eye can see.
I'll drink to that.
Hrrrnnn.
BE-DOOP!
I think I have something.

Find the kid?

Uh-huh. The last command line here was a directive activating a group of bounty hunters. *And* while they were operating under a kill order...

Which is always sexy...

he interesting thing s the search query the directive was attached to.

Take a look:

They were, indeed, hunting the **Great Beast.**

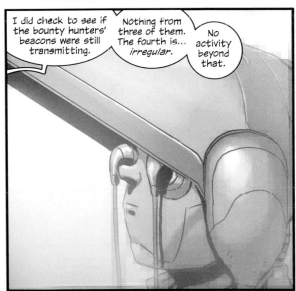

I did check to see if the bounty hunters' beacons were still transmitting.

Nothing from three of them. The fourth is... *irregular.*

No activity beyond that.

Well...

Sounds like we have some catching up to do.

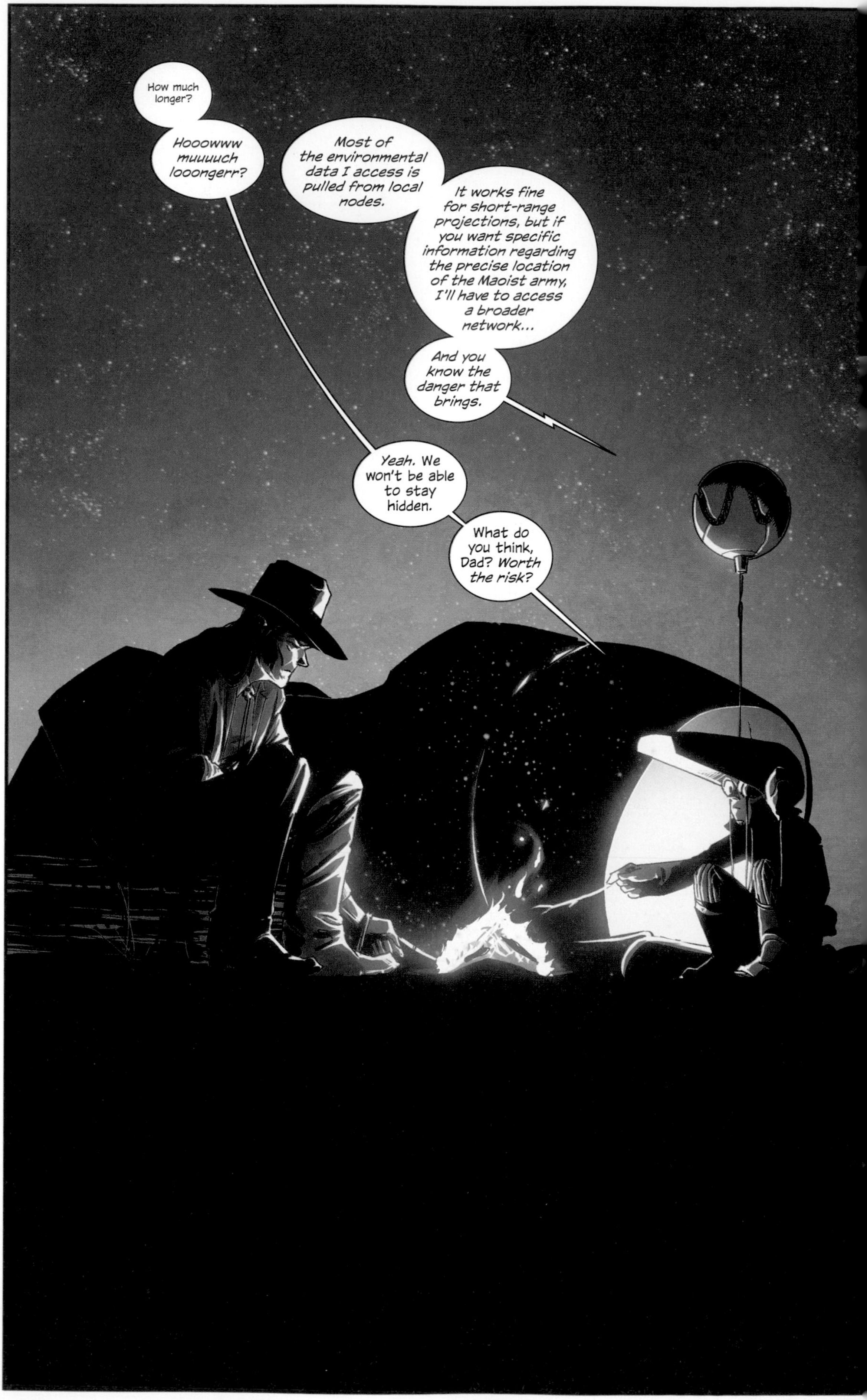
How much longer?
Hooowww muuuuch looongerr?
Most of the environmental data I access is pulled from local nodes.
It works fine for short-range projections, but if you want specific information regarding the precise location of the Maoist army, I'll have to access a broader network...
And you know the danger that brings.
Yeah. We won't be able to stay hidden.
What do you think, Dad? Worth the risk?

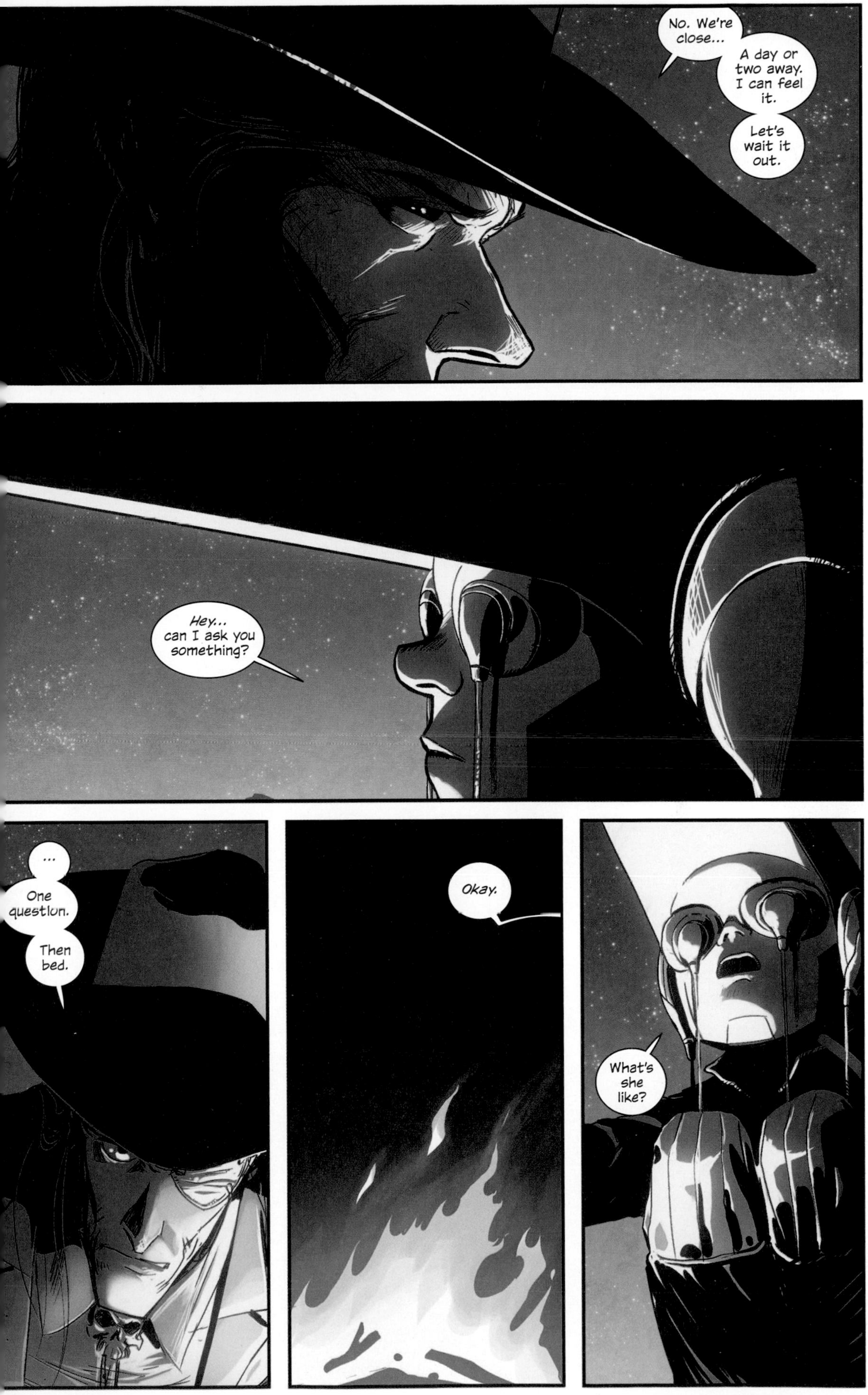
No. We're close...
A day or two away. I can feel it.
Let's wait it out.
Hey... can I ask you something?
...
One question.
Then bed.
Okay.
What's she like?

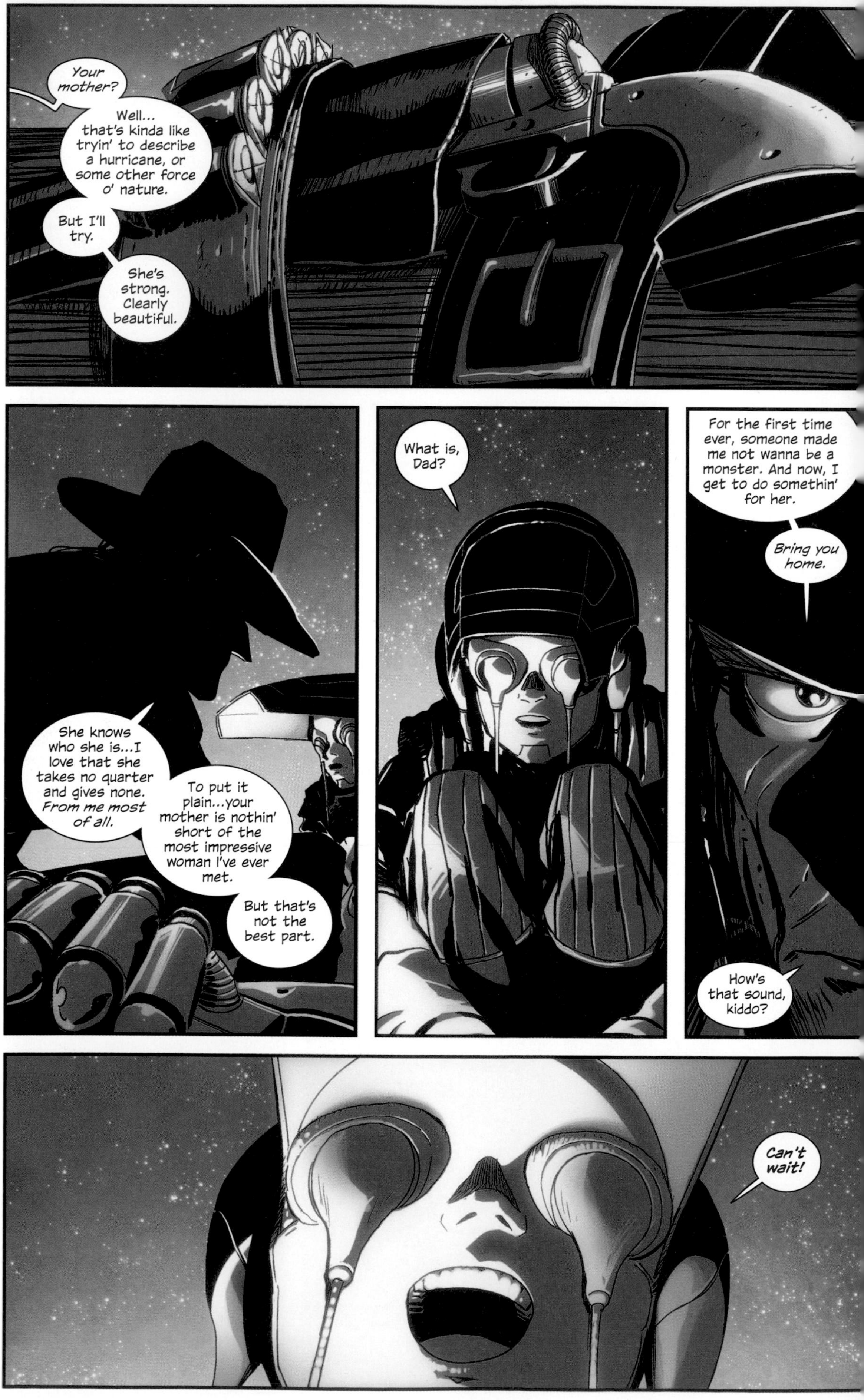
Your mother?
Well... that's kinda like tryin' to describe a hurricane, or some other force o' nature.
But I'll try.
She's strong. Clearly beautiful.
She knows who she is...I love that she takes no quarter and gives none. *From me most of all.*
To put it plain...your mother is nothin' short of the most impressive woman I've ever met.
But that's not the best part.
What is, Dad?
For the first time ever, someone made me not wanna be a monster. And now, I get to do somethin' for her.
Bring you home.
How's that sound, kiddo?
Can't wait!

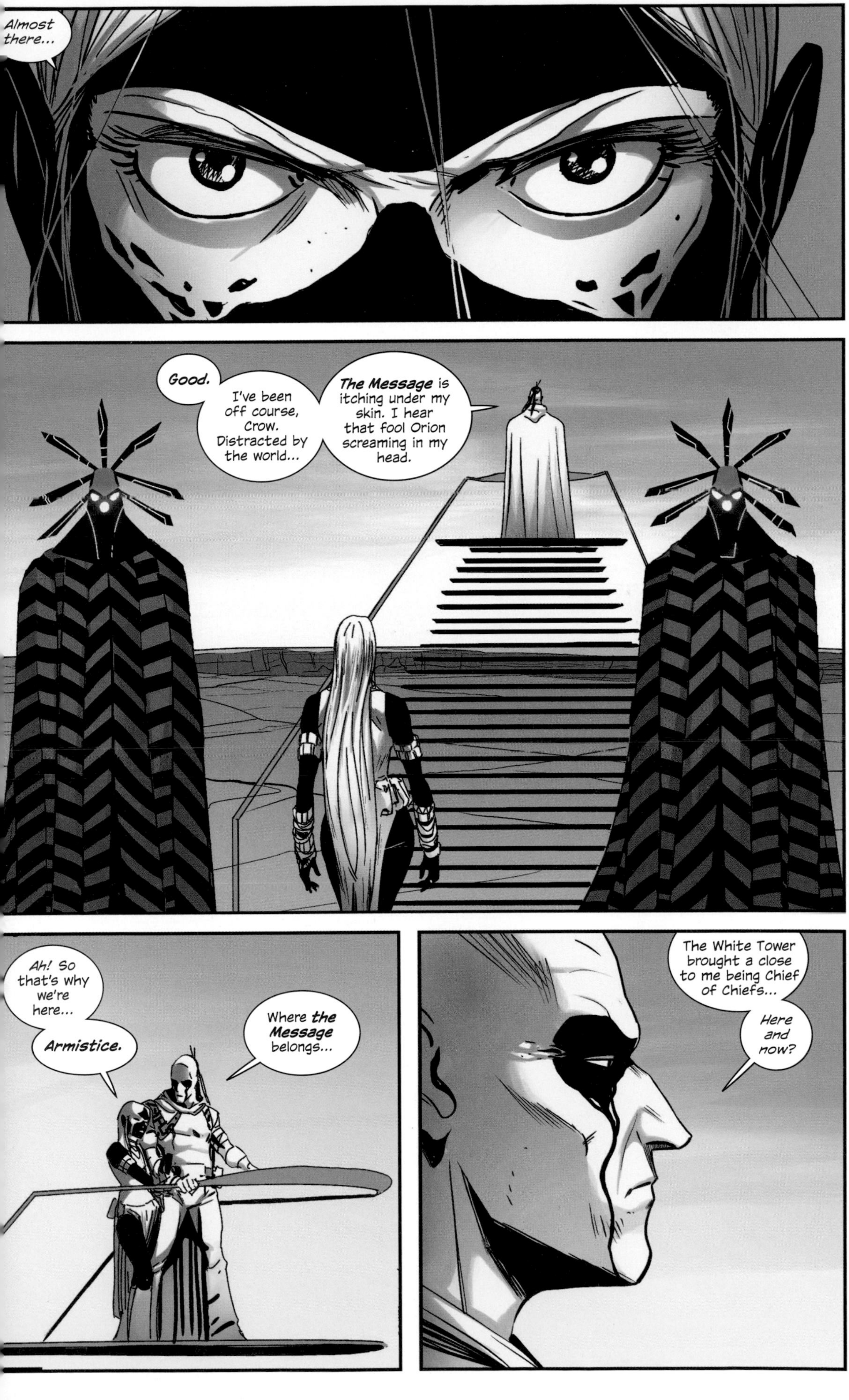
Almost there...
Good.
I've been off course, Crow. Distracted by the world...
The Message is itching under my skin. I hear that fool Orion screaming in my head.
Ah! So that's why we're here...
Armistice.
Where the Message belongs...
The White Tower brought a close to me being Chief of Chiefs...
Here and now?

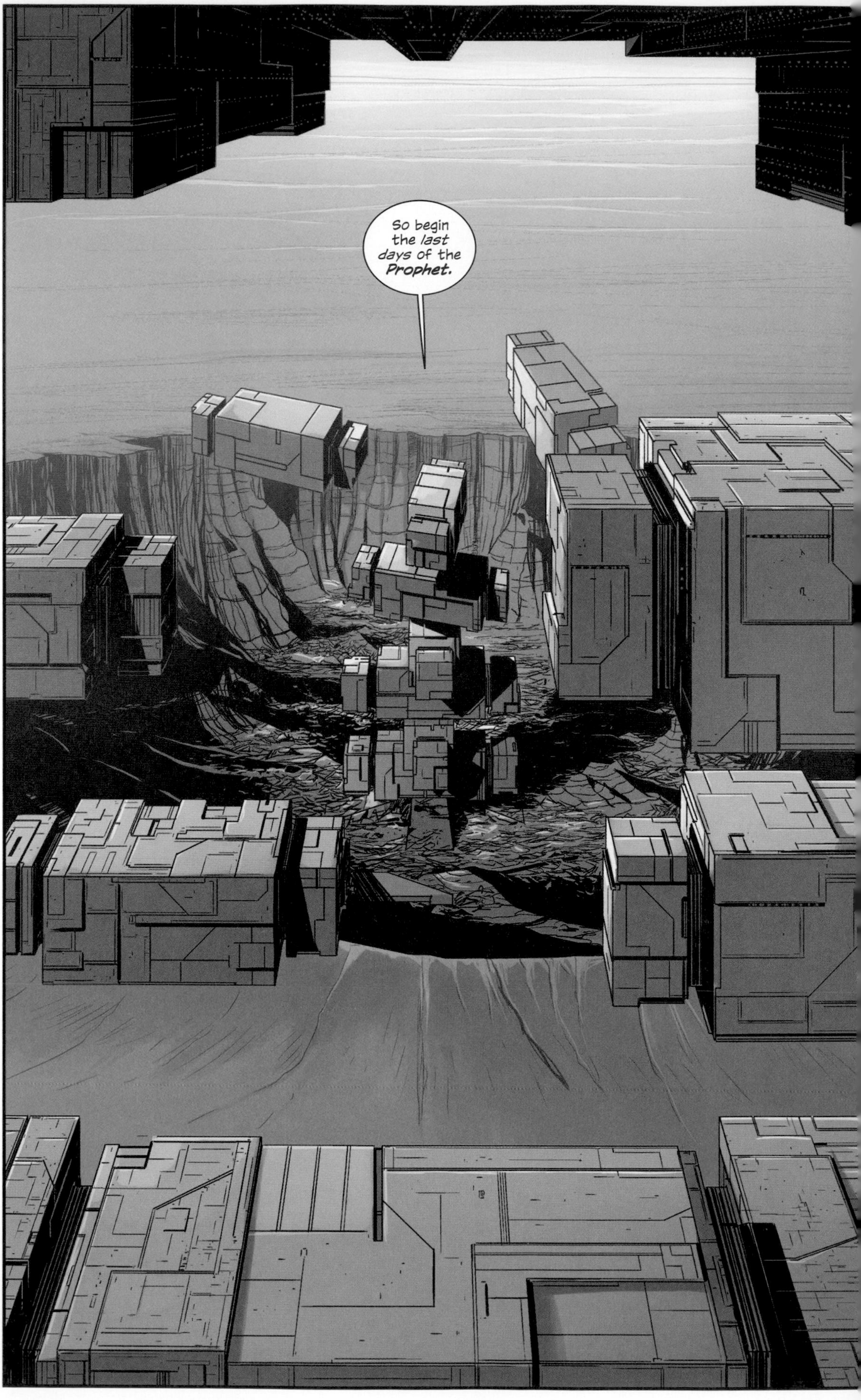
So begin the *last* days of the **Prophet.**

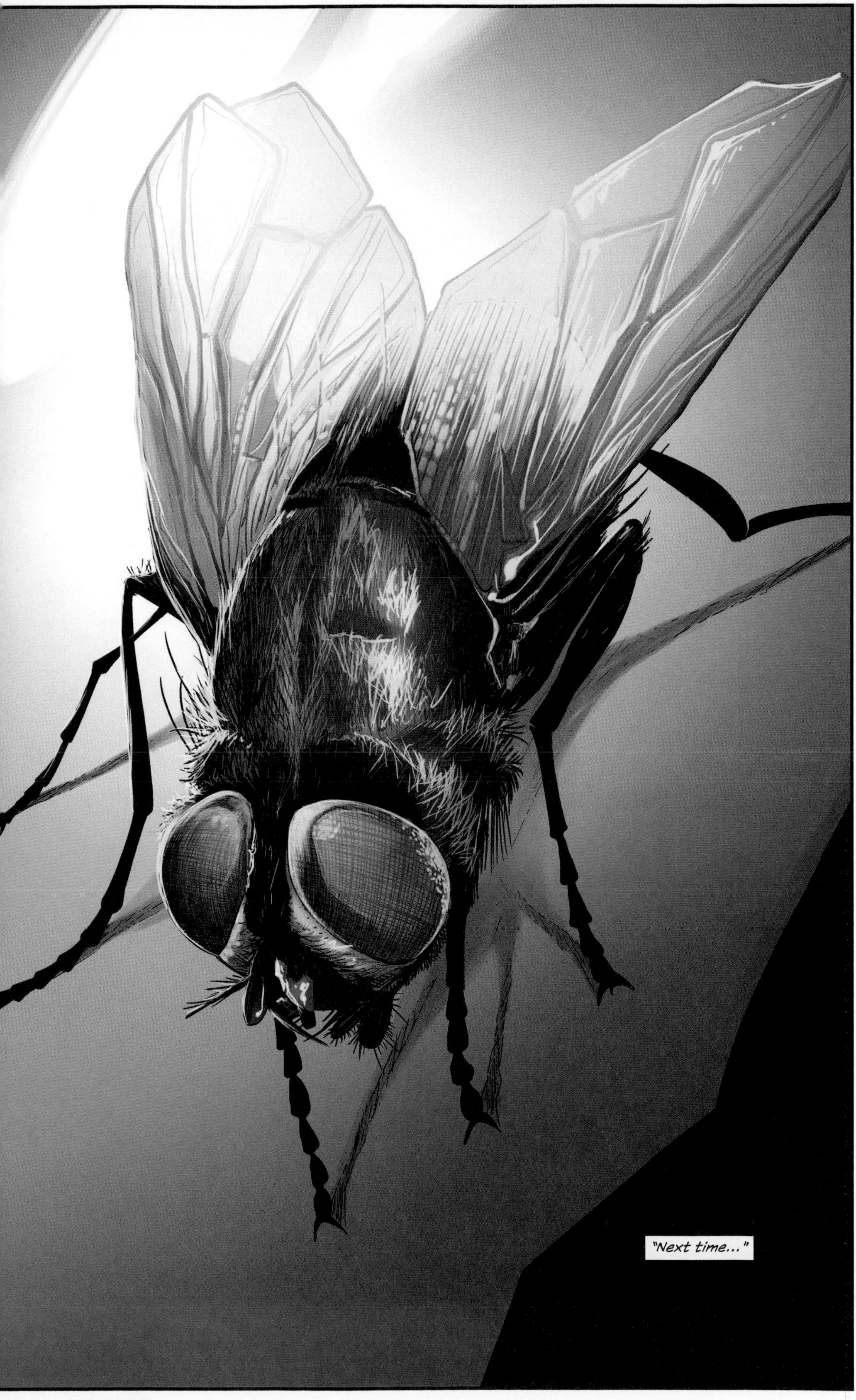
"Next time..."

"You might want to be a bit more appreciative when a man like myself is feeling generous."
"Understand?"
"You--you..."
"Do-do your worst."
Happy to oblige.
BLAM! BLAM!
ACHHKKKKK!

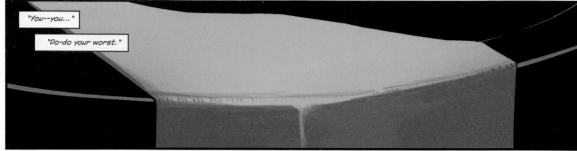

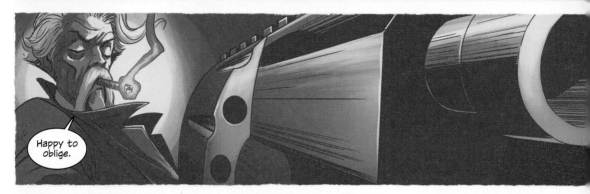

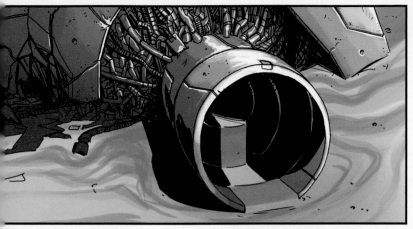

Damn you.

Hrnnnnn.

Huff.

Huff.

Huff.

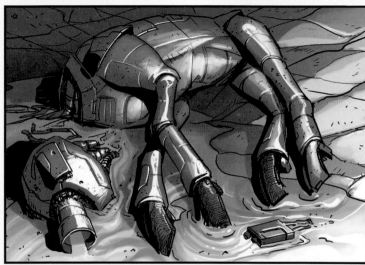

Hrnnnnn.

RSHHHHT!

Hrnnnnn.

Huff.

Huff.

Hrnnnnn.

Huff.

Huff.

RED

VWWWRRRR

I ASKED FOR **MERCY**,
I SETTLED FOR **JUSTICE**,
NOW ALL THAT REMAINS IS
REVENGE.

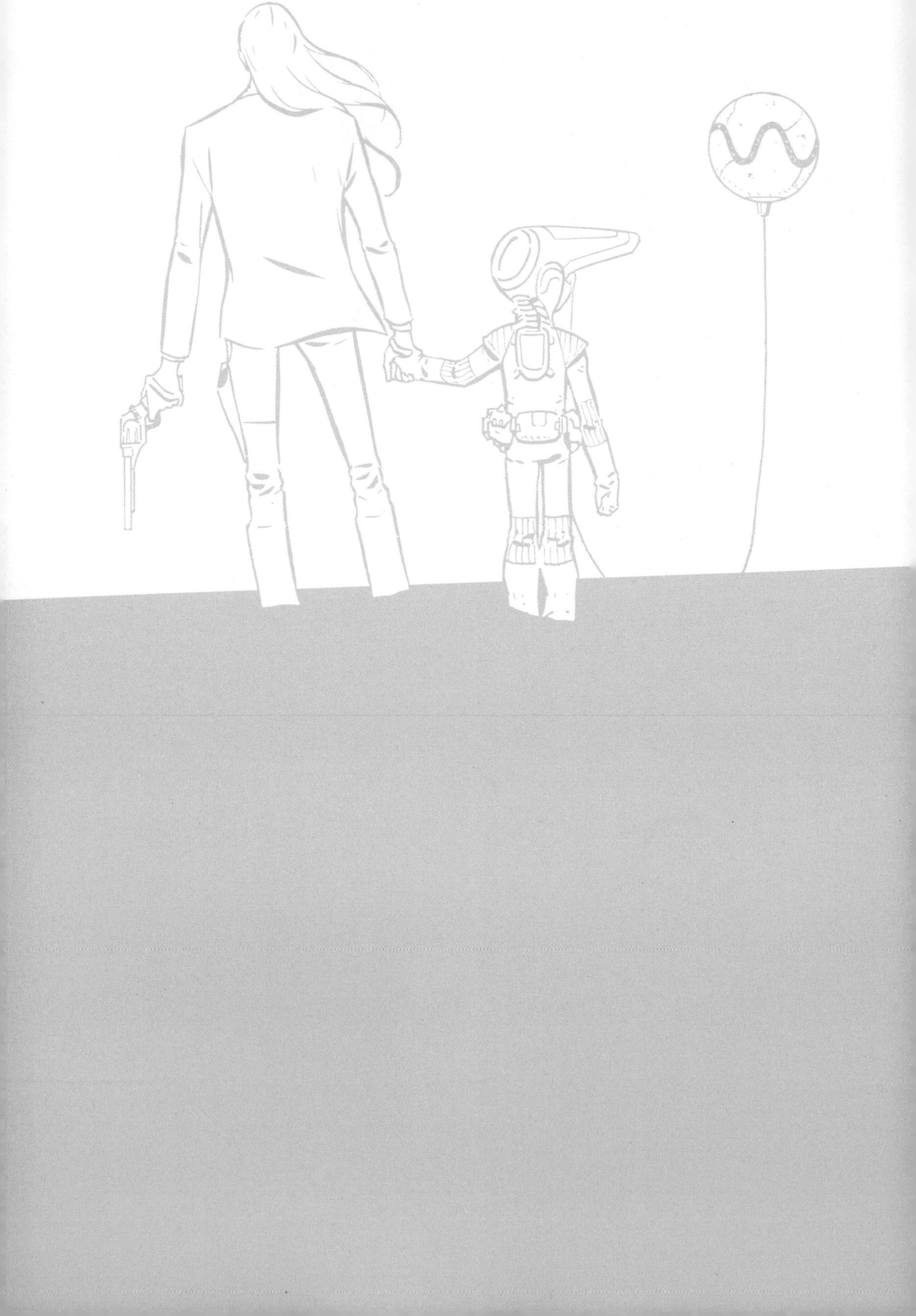

37

 THIRTY-SEVEN:
THE **HUNT** IS **ON**

IF I AM NOT **VENGEANCE,**
THEN I AM **NOTHING.**

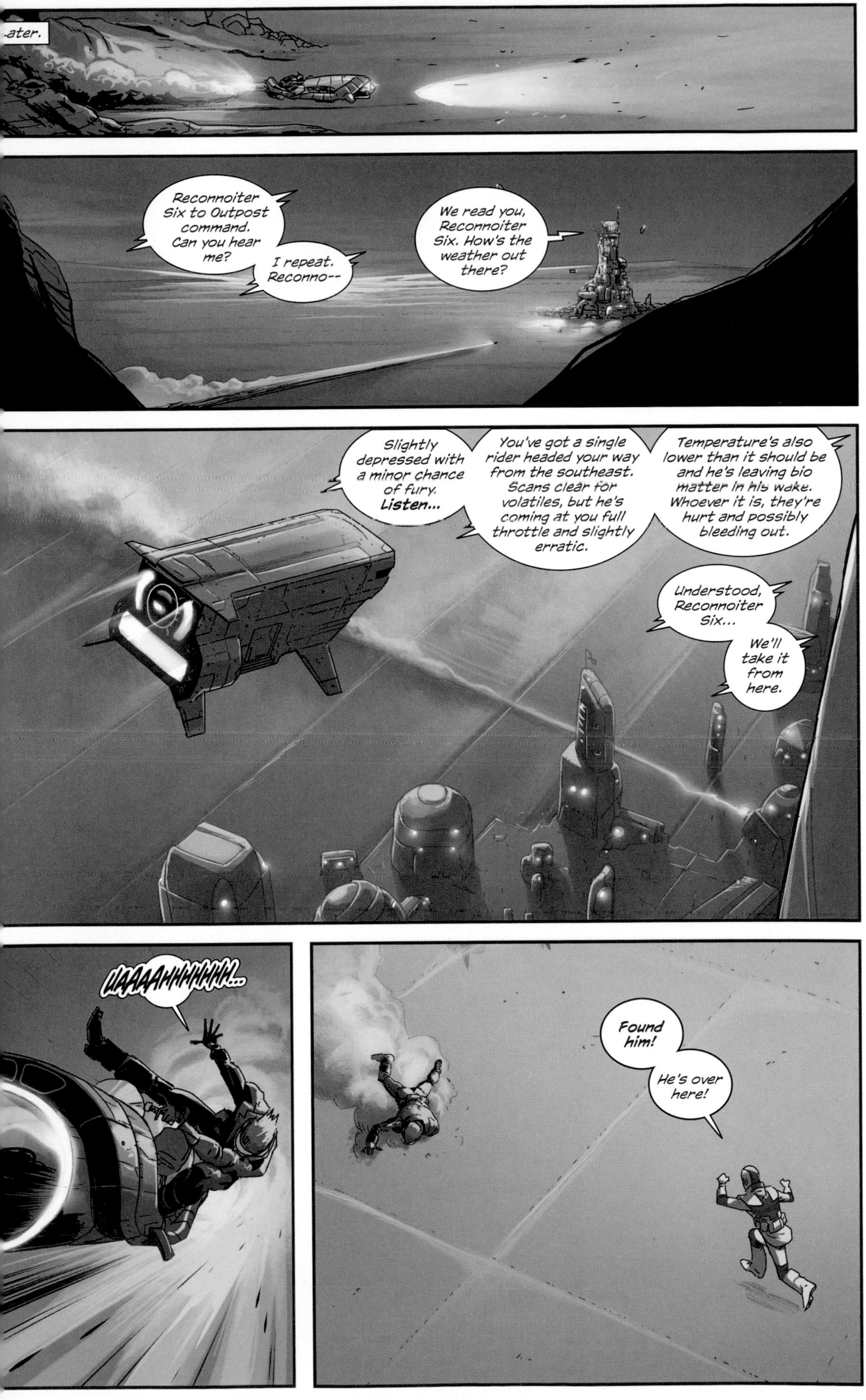
ater.
Reconnoiter Six to Outpost command. Can you hear me?
I repeat. Reconno--
We read you, Reconnoiter Six. How's the weather out there?
Slightly depressed with a minor chance of fury. **Listen...**
You've got a single rider headed your way from the southeast. Scans clear for volatiles, but he's coming at you full throttle and slightly erratic.
Temperature's also lower than it should be and he's leaving bio matter in his wake. Whoever it is, they're hurt and possibly bleeding out.
Understood, Reconnoiter Six...
We'll take it from here.
UAAAAHHHHHHH...
Found him!
He's over here!

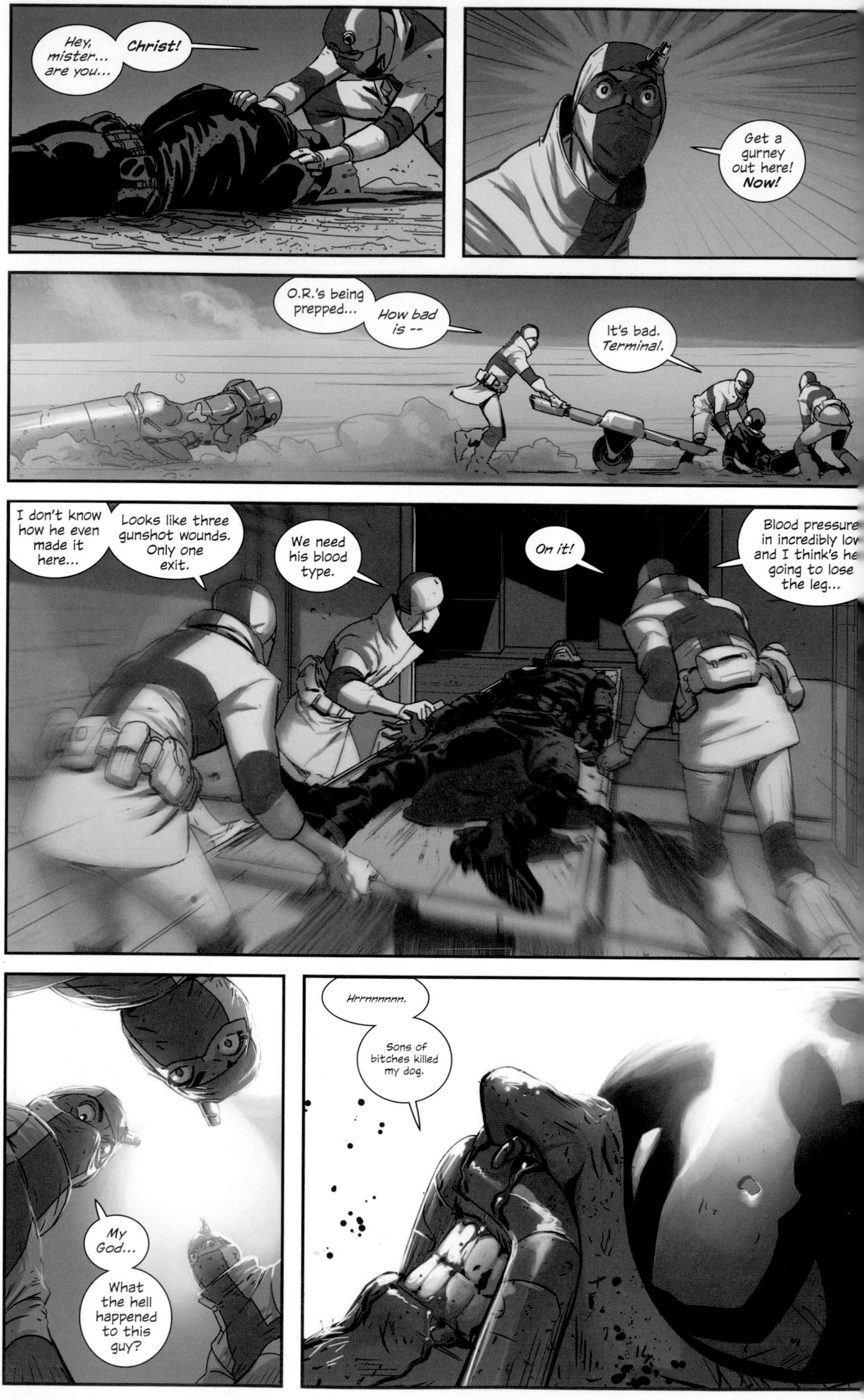
Hey, mister... are you...
Christ!
Get a gurney out here! Now!
O.R.'s being prepped...
How bad is --
It's bad. Terminal.
I don't know how he even made it here...
Looks like three gunshot wounds. Only one exit.
We need his blood type.
On it!
Blood pressure in incredibly low and I think's he going to lose the leg...
My God...
What the hell happened to this guy?
Hrrnnnnnn.
Sons of bitches killed my dog.

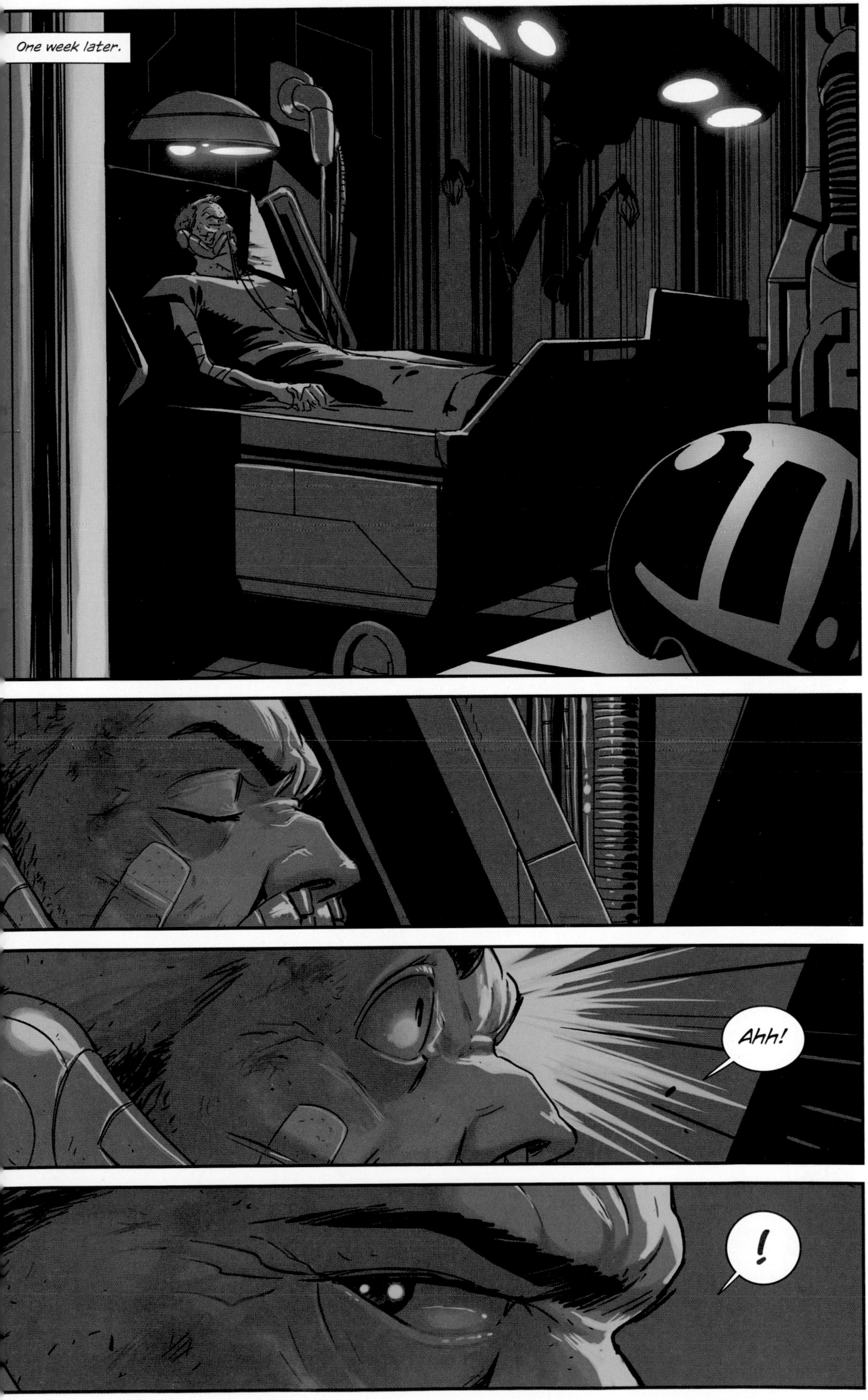
One week later.
Ahh!
!

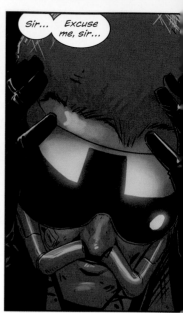

Sir... Excuse me, sir...

I'm not sure you should be out of bed, are you...

Are you all right?

No. I am not.

Would you like me to get you--

No. You ain't got nothin' I need.

So--so what do you need?

An ambulance.

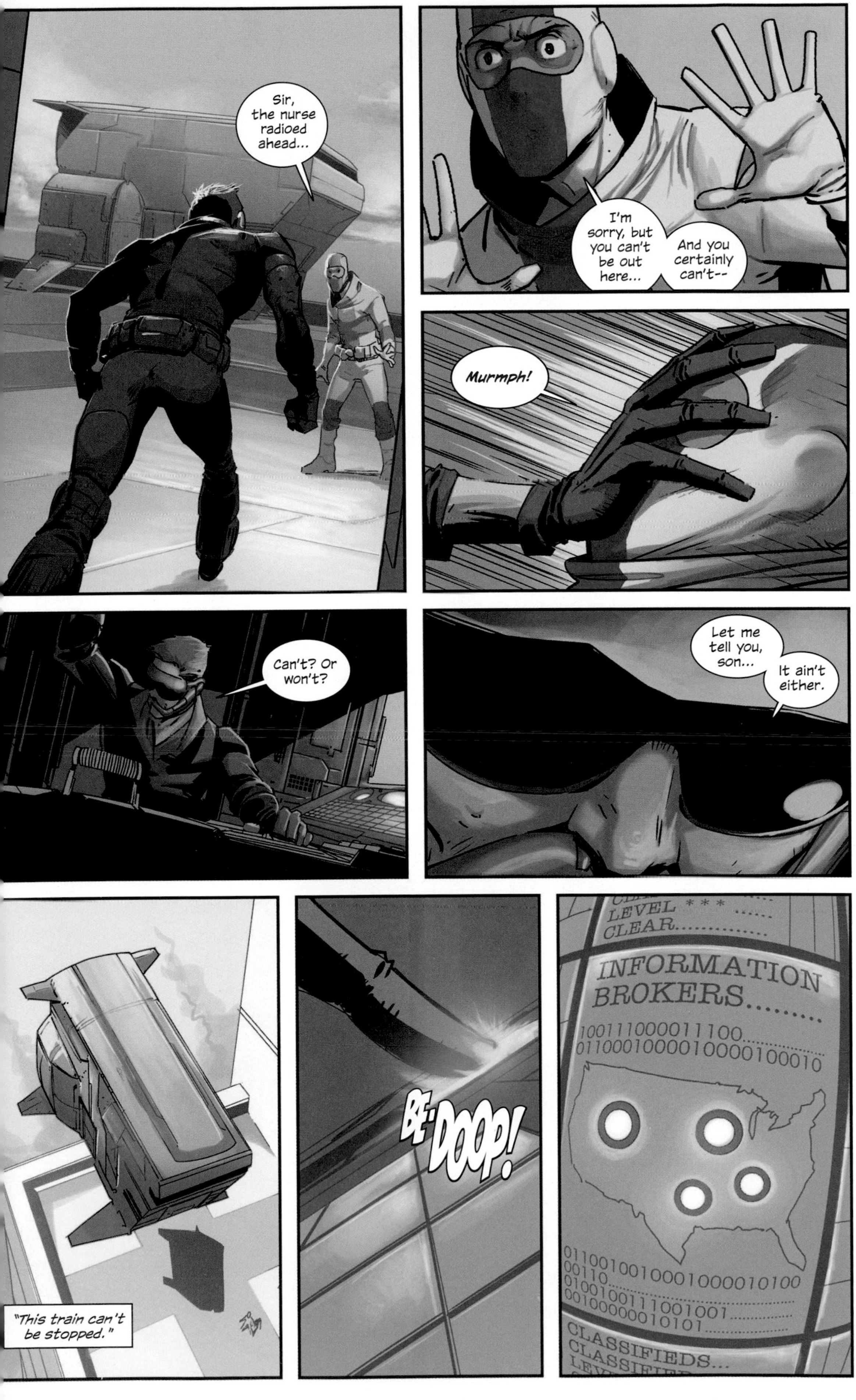
Sir, the nurse radioed ahead...
I'm sorry, but you can't be out here...
And you certainly can't--
Murmph!
Can't? Or won't?
Let me tell you, son...
It ain't either.
"This train can't be stopped."
BE-DOOP!
LEVEL * * *
CLEAR
INFORMATION BROKERS
100111000011100
0110001000010000100010
0110010010001000010100
00110
0100100111001001
0010000000010101
CLASSIFIEDS
CLASSIFIEDS...

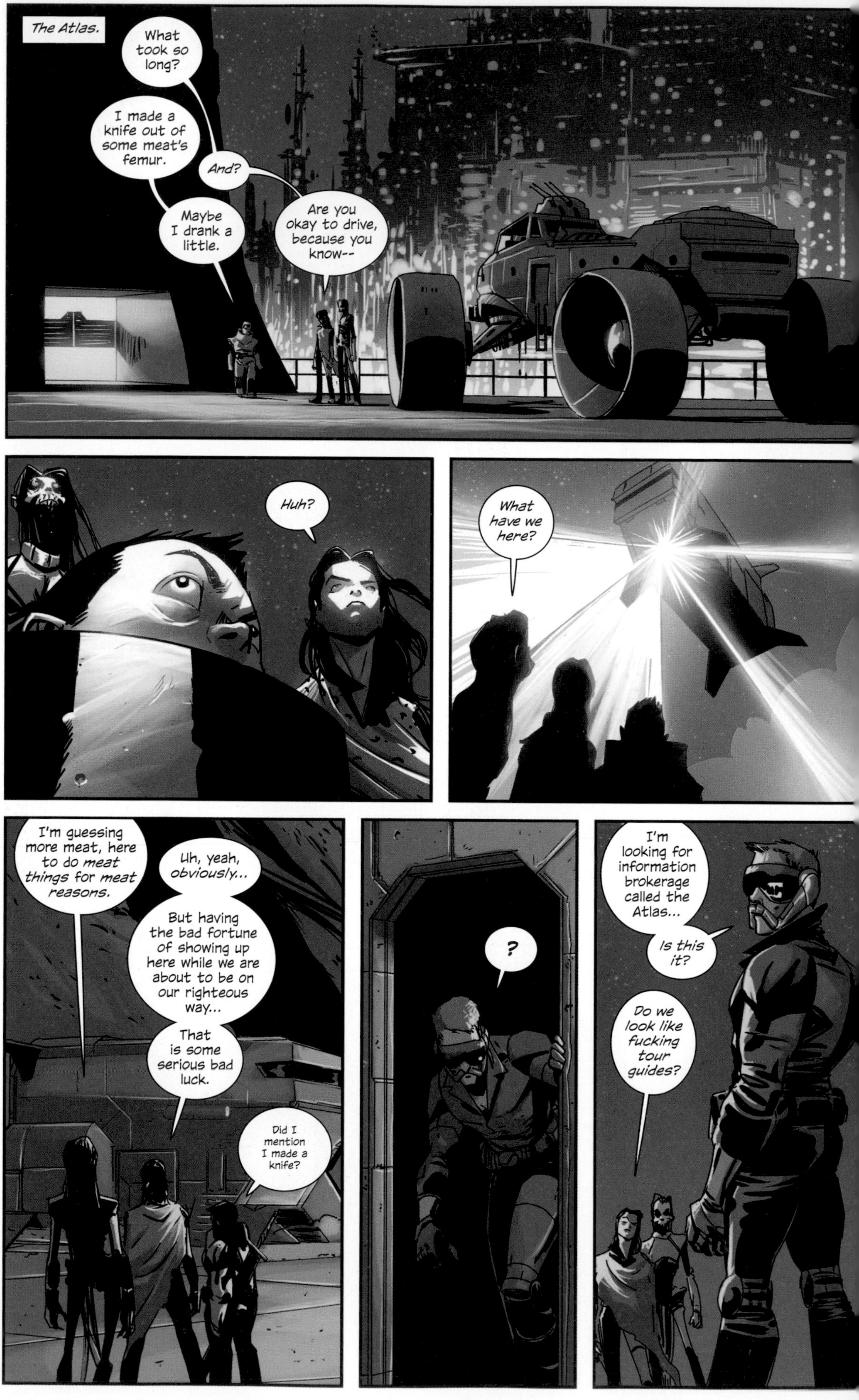
The Atlas.
What took so long?
I made a knife out of some meat's femur.
And?
Maybe I drank a little.
Are you okay to drive, because you know--
Huh?
What have we here?
I'm guessing more meat, here to do *meat* things for *meat* reasons.
Uh, yeah, *obviously*...
But having the bad fortune of showing up here while we are about to be on our righteous way...
That is some serious bad luck.
Did I mention I made a knife?
?
I'm looking for information brokerage called the Atlas...
Is this it?
Do we look like fucking tour guides?

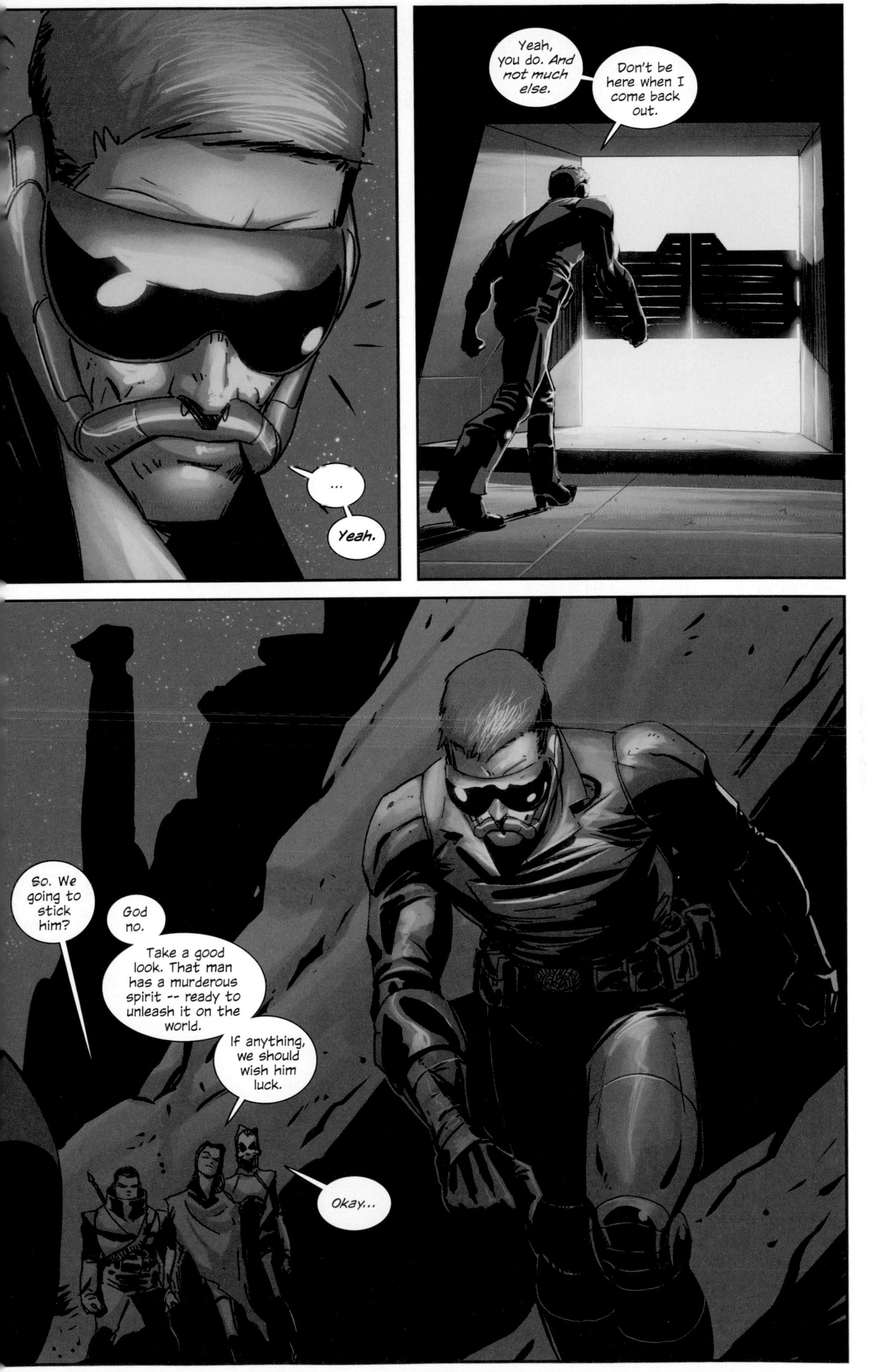
...
Yeah.
Yeah, you do. And not much else.
Don't be here when I come back out.
So. We going to stick him?
God no.
Take a good look. That man has a murderous spirit -- ready to unleash it on the world.
If anything, we should wish him luck.
Okay...

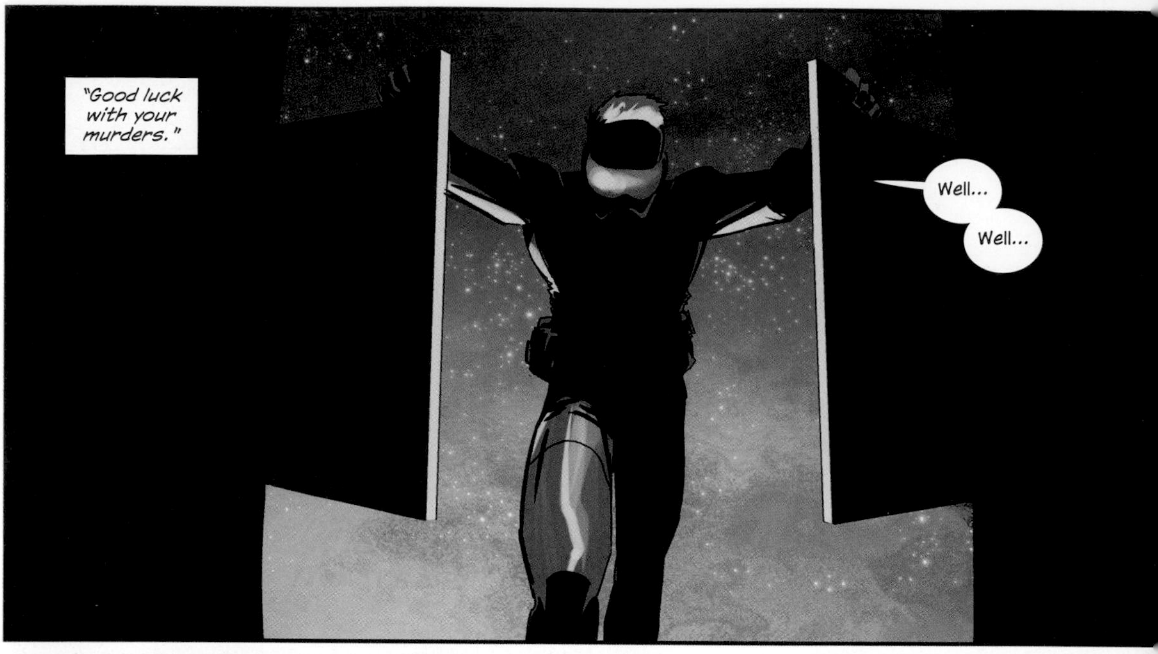
"Good luck with your murders."
Well...
Well...

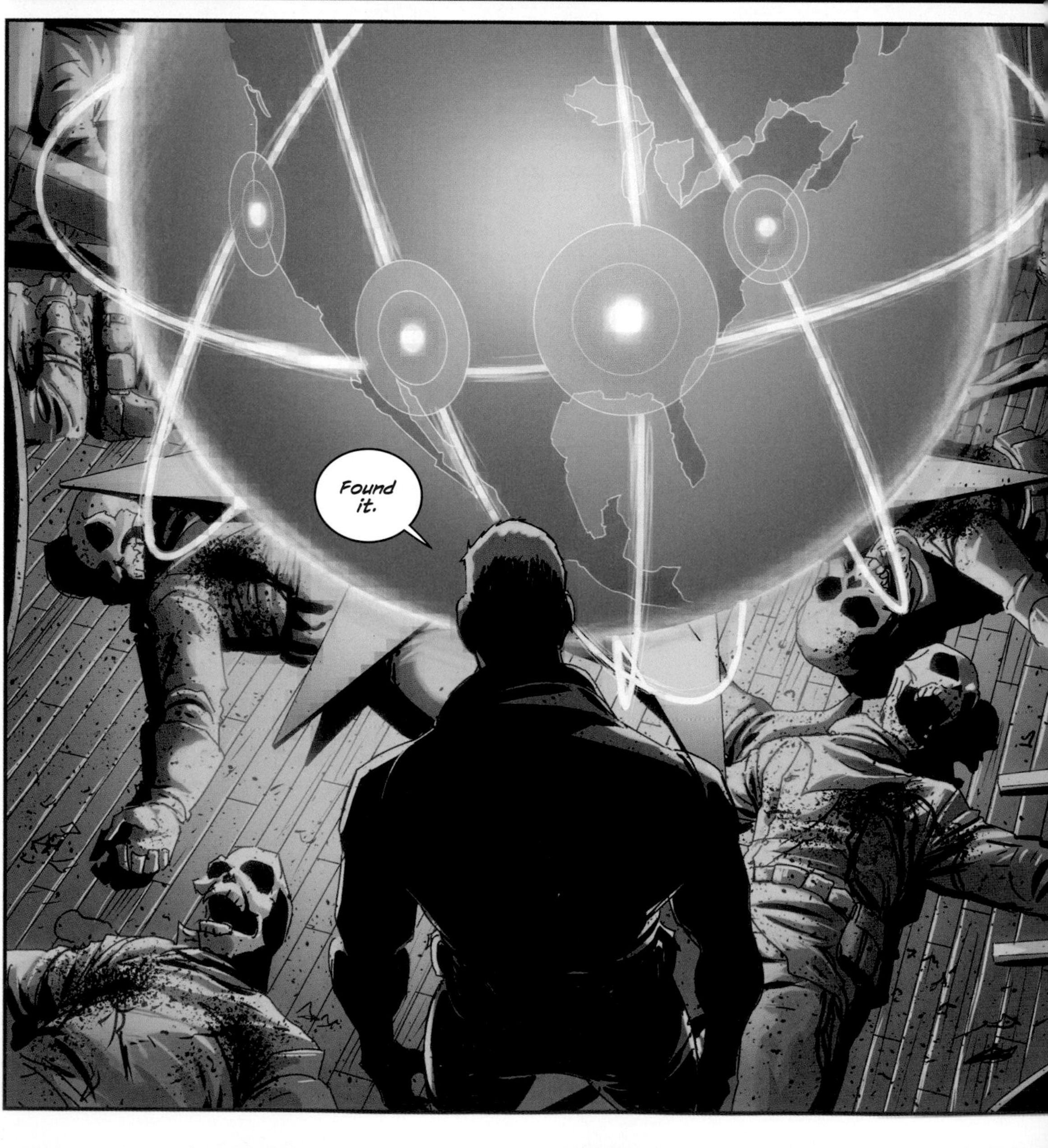
Found it.

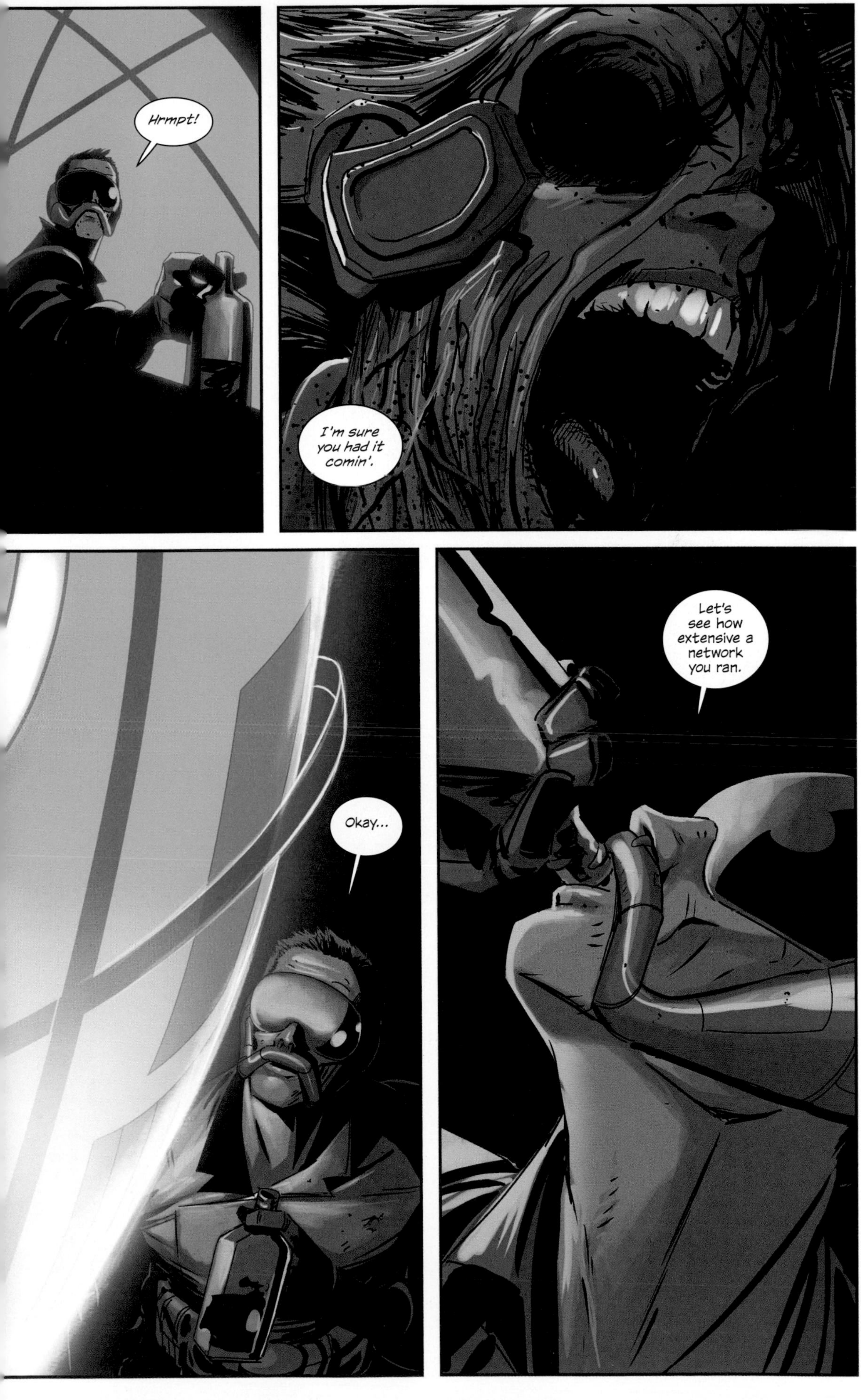
Hrmpt!
I'm sure you had it comin'.
Okay...
Let's see how extensive a network you ran.

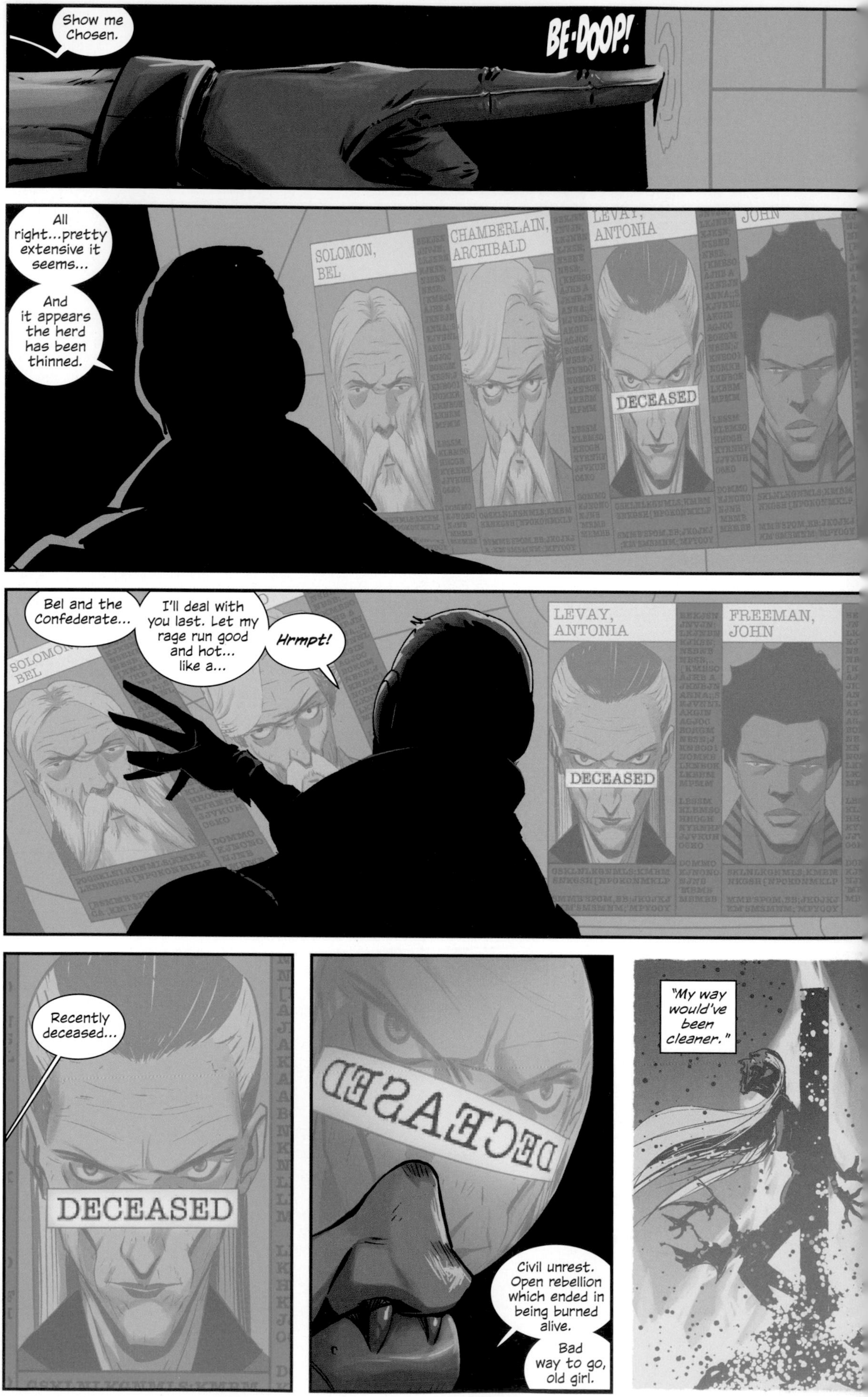
Show me Chosen.
BE-DOOP!
All right...pretty extensive it seems...
And it appears the herd has been thinned.
SOLOMON, BEL
CHAMBERLAIN, ARCHIBALD
LEVAY, ANTONIA
DECEASED
JOHN
Bel and the Confederate...
I'll deal with you last. Let my rage run good and hot... like a...
Hrmpt!
SOLOMON, BEL
LEVAY, ANTONIA
DECEASED
FREEMAN, JOHN
Recently deceased...
DECEASED
DECEASED
Civil unrest. Open rebellion which ended in being burned alive.
Bad way to go, old girl.
"My way would've been cleaner."

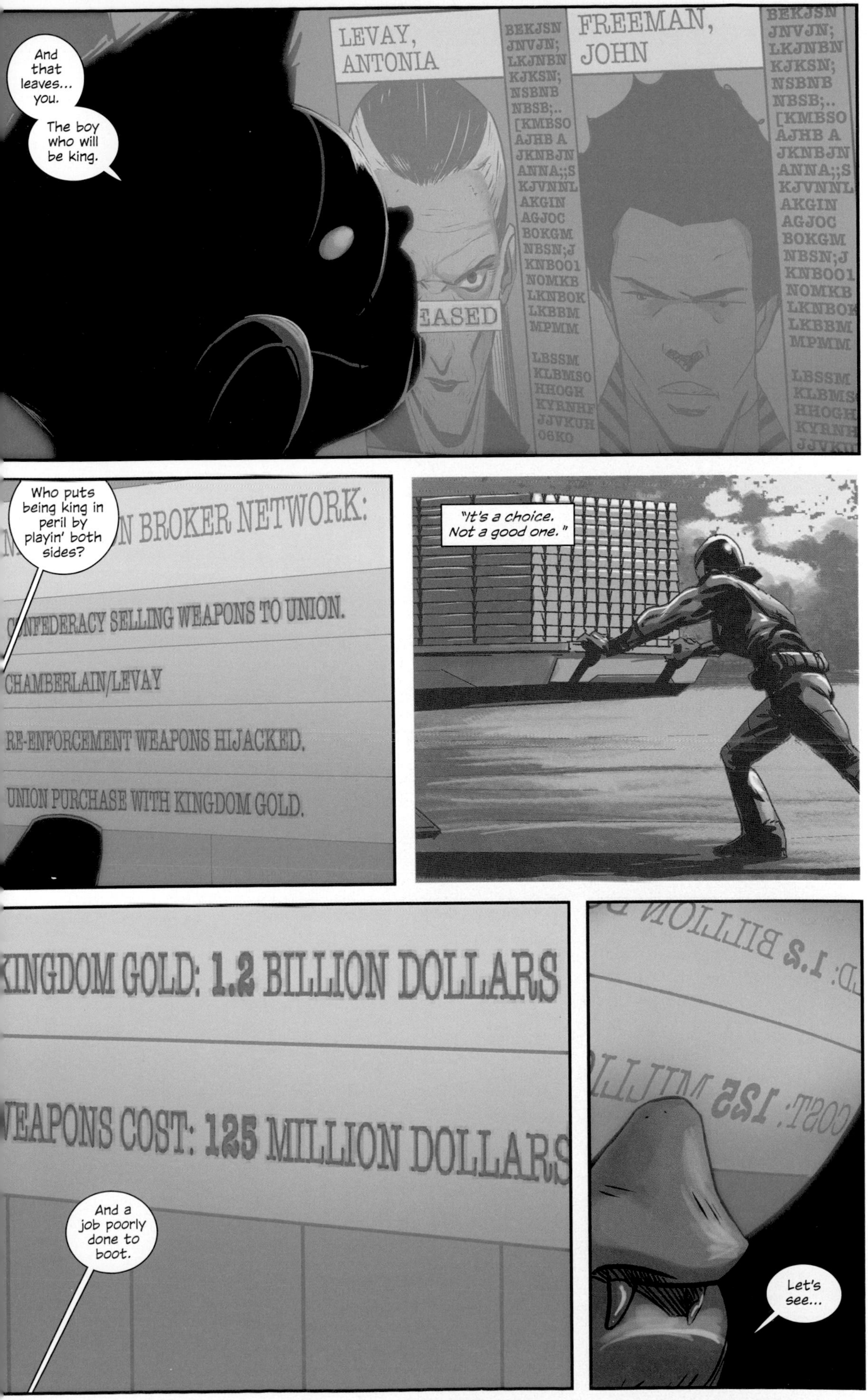
And that leaves... you.
The boy who will be king.
LEVAY, ANTONIA
FREEMAN, JOHN
Who puts being king in peril by playin' both sides?
BROKER NETWORK:
CONFEDERACY SELLING WEAPONS TO UNION.
CHAMBERLAIN/LEVAY
RE-ENFORCEMENT WEAPONS HIJACKED.
UNION PURCHASE WITH KINGDOM GOLD.
"It's a choice. Not a good one."
KINGDOM GOLD: 1.2 BILLION DOLLARS
WEAPONS COST: 125 MILLION DOLLARS
And a job poorly done to boot.
Let's see...

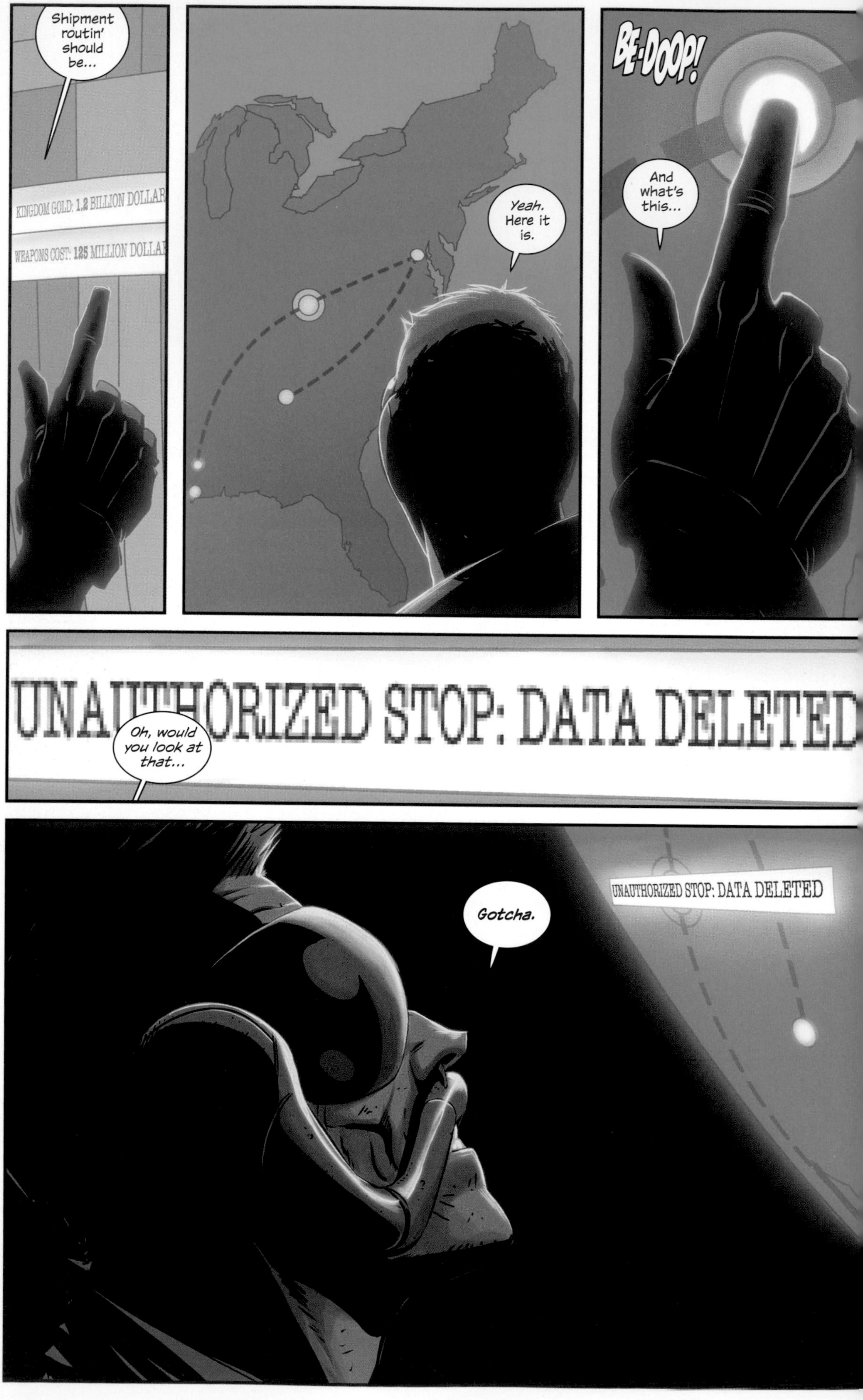
Shipment routin' should be...
KINGDOM GOLD: 1.2 BILLION DOLLAR
WEAPONS COST: 125 MILLION DOLLA
Yeah. Here it is.
BE-DOOP!
And what's this...
UNAUTHORIZED STOP: DATA DELETED
Oh, would you look at that...
UNAUTHORIZED STOP: DATA DELETED
Gotcha.

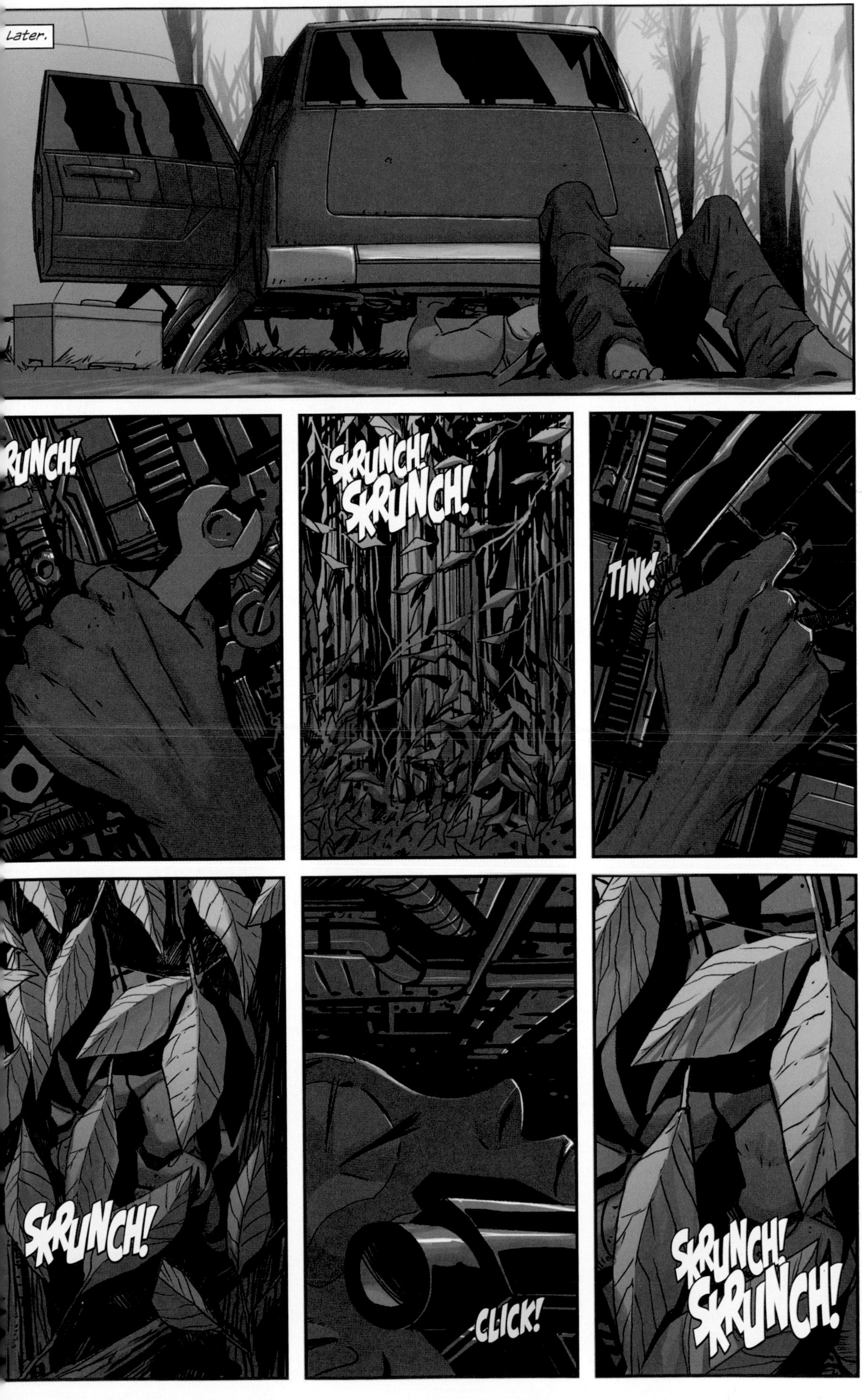
Later.
RUNCH!
SKRUNCH!
SKRUNCH!
TINK!
SKRUNCH!
CLICK!
SKRUNCH!
SKRUNCH!

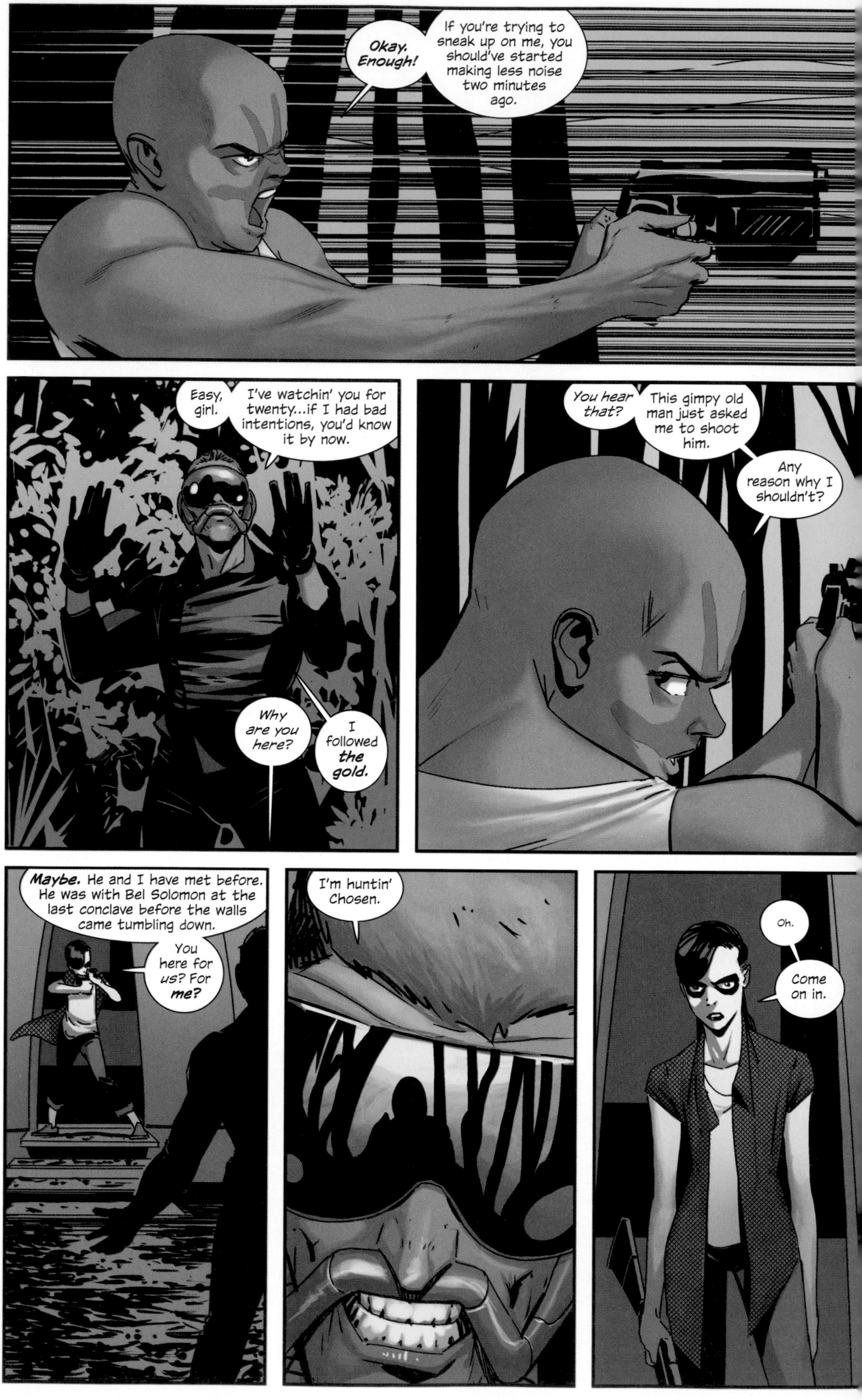

Okay. Enough!
If you're trying to sneak up on me, you should've started making less noise two minutes ago.
Easy, girl.
I've watchin' you for twenty...if I had bad intentions, you'd know it by now.
Why are you here?
I followed the gold.
You hear that?
This gimpy old man just asked me to shoot him.
Any reason why I shouldn't?
Maybe. He and I have met before. He was with Bel Solomon at the last conclave before the walls came tumbling down.
You here for us? For me?
I'm huntin' Chosen.
Oh.
Come on in.

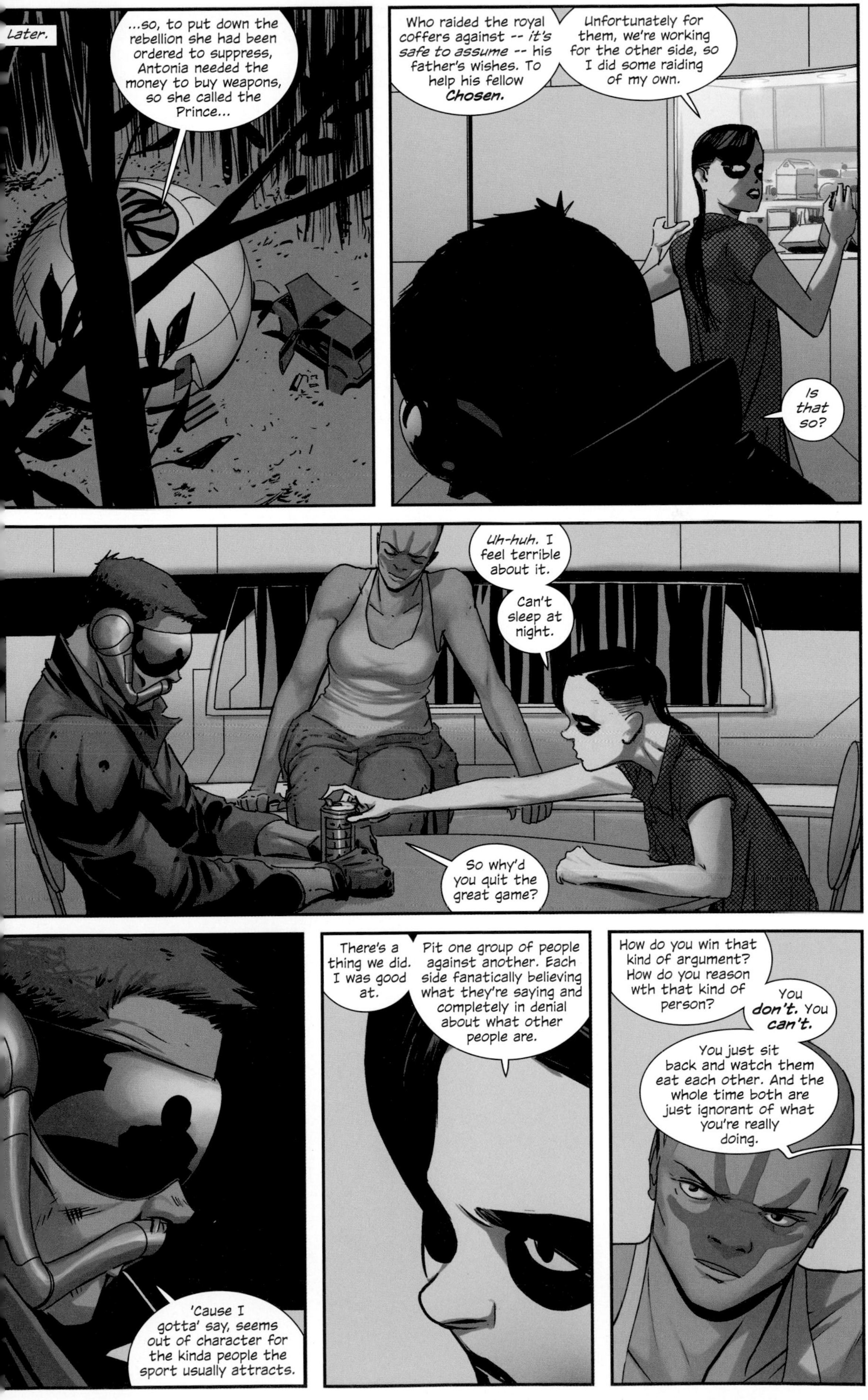
Later.
...so, to put down the rebellion she had been ordered to suppress, Antonia needed the money to buy weapons, so she called the Prince...
Who raided the royal coffers against -- *it's safe to assume* -- his father's wishes. To help his fellow ***Chosen.***
Unfortunately for them, we're working for the other side, so I did some raiding of my own.
Is that so?
Uh-huh. I feel terrible about it.
Can't sleep at night.
So why'd you quit the great game?
'Cause I gotta' say, seems out of character for the kinda people the sport usually attracts.
There's a thing we did. I was good at.
Pit one group of people against another. Each side fanatically believing what they're saying and completely in denial about what other people are.
How do you win that kind of argument? How do you reason wth that kind of person?
You ***don't.*** You ***can't.***
You just sit back and watch them eat each other. And the whole time both are just ignorant of what you're really doing.

I admit, I found the influence -- *the power* -- intoxicating...but then I saw how quickly I was abandoned, and...*well*, it's sobering.

I thought I mattered, but I was just another another piece on the board.

Anything else?

No. That'll do.

It's enough.

So... you're going to just march right into the Kingdom and beat the Prince to death with your bare hands.

That's your plan?

You gotta better idea?

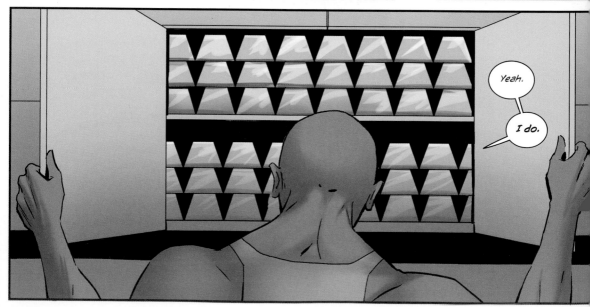

Yeah.

I do.

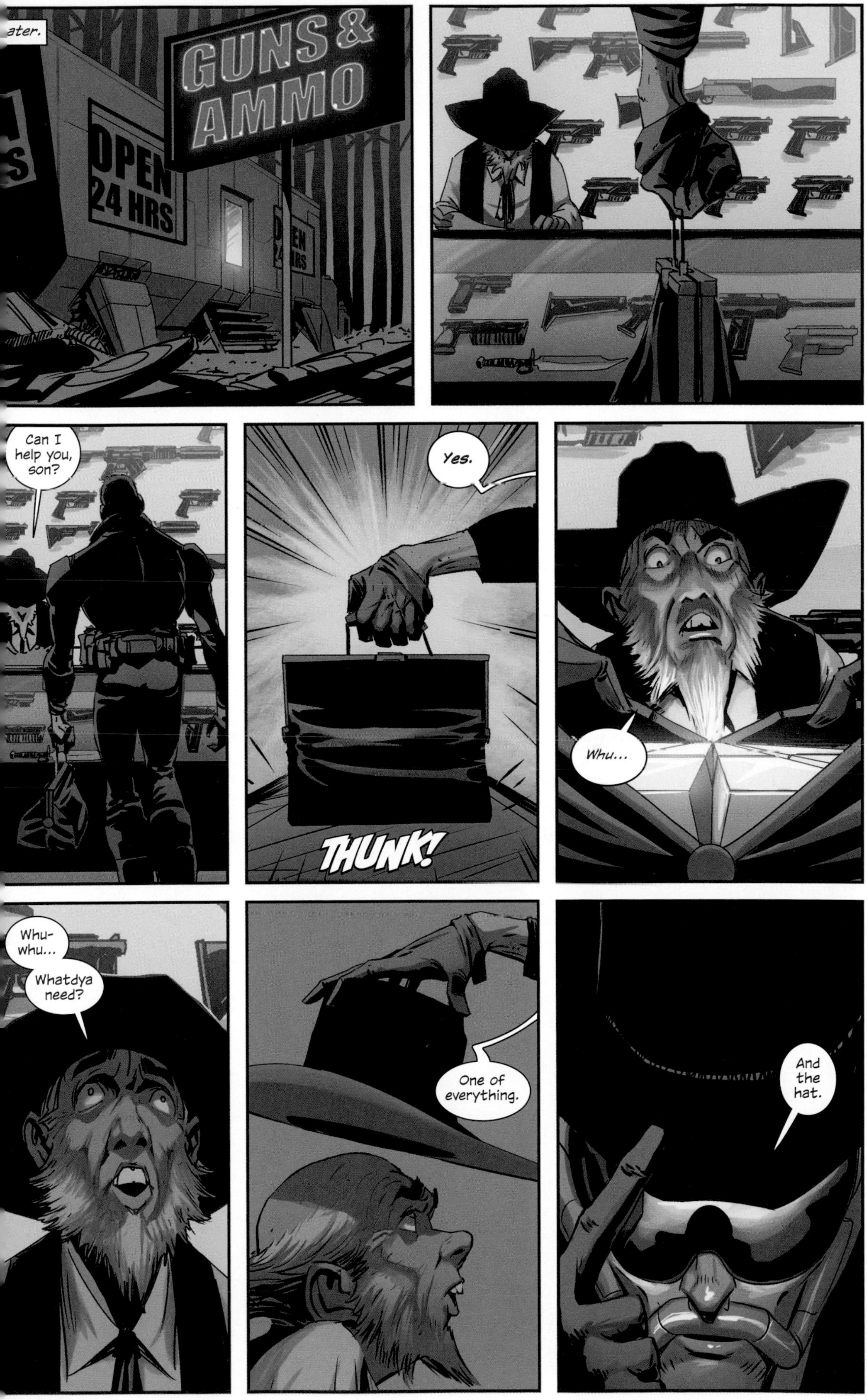
ater.
GUNS & AMMO
OPEN 24 HRS
OPEN 24 HRS
Can I help you, son?
Yes.
THUNK!
Whu...
Whu-whu...
Whatdya need?
One of everything.
And the hat.

Later.
CH-CHHUNNK!

CH-CHHUNNK!
CH-CHHUNNK!
CH-CHHUNNK!
CH-CHHUNNK!

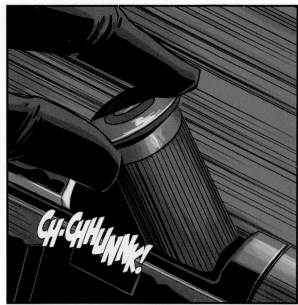

CH-CHHUNNK!

Well, this is it...

BLiR

Time to say goodnight, sweet prince.

I'm gonna close those eyes...

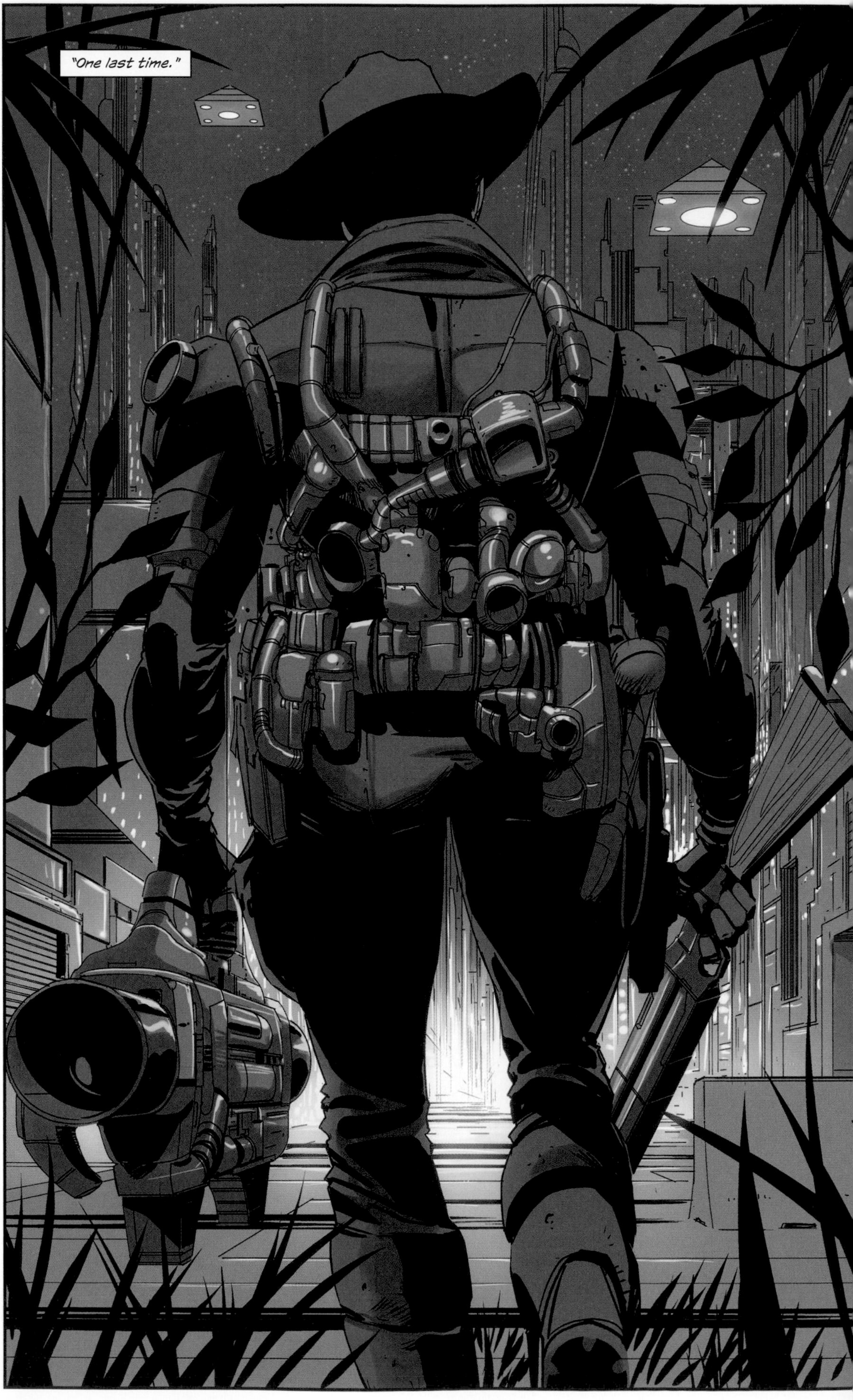
"One last time."

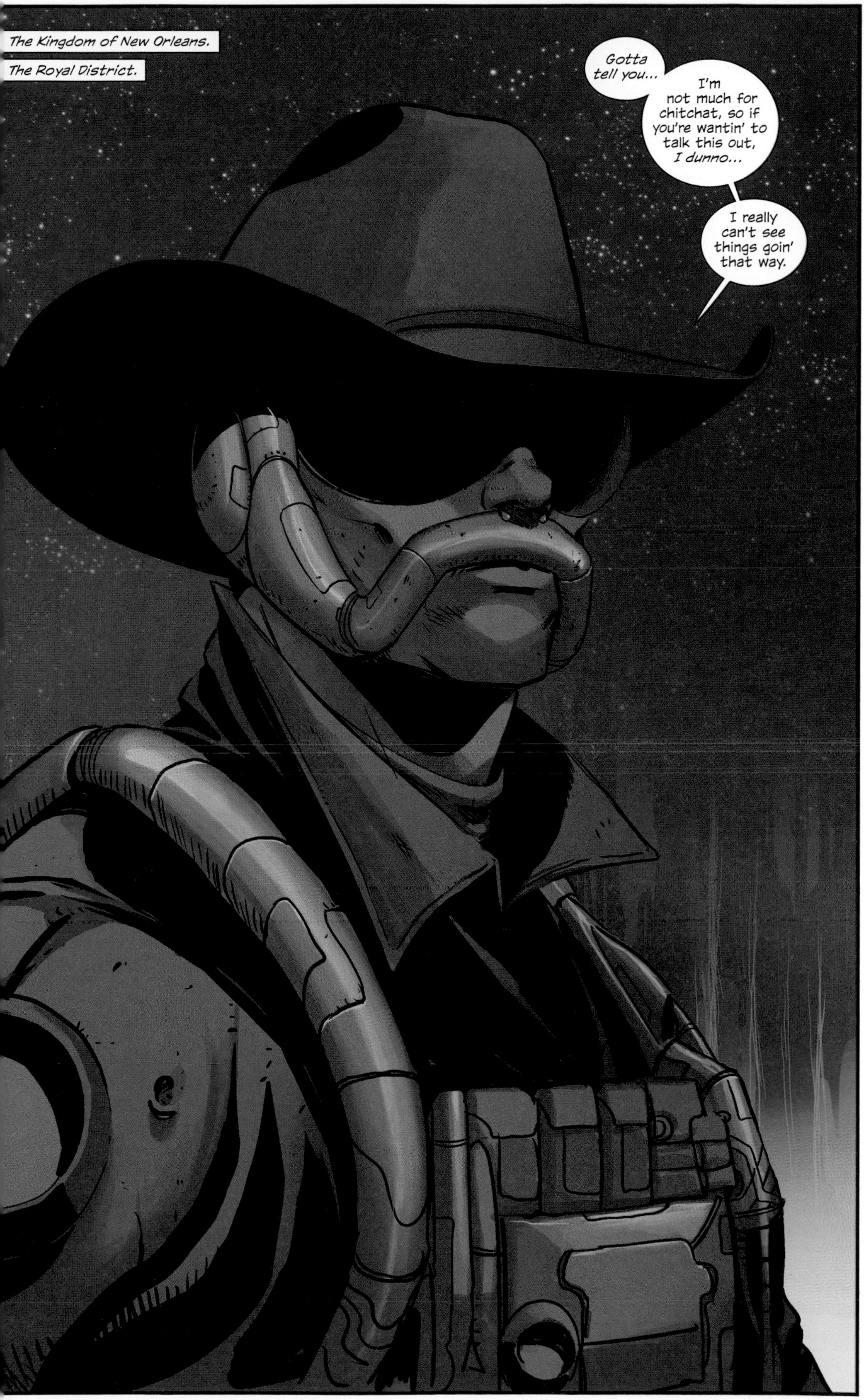
The Kingdom of New Orleans.
The Royal District.
Gotta tell you...
I'm not much for chitchat, so if you're wantin' to talk this out, I dunno...
I really can't see things goin' that way.

Old man... do you seriously think anyone here is interested in *stimulating* conversation?

Yeah.

I do.

'Cause I've spent years starin' down **bad men** with death in their eyes who wanted nothin' more than to see me *buried* and gone.

To think I don't know the difference between **that** and a buncha *well-dressed*, *soft boys* playin' **hard** at bein' **hard** is an insult to everything I am.

Heh. All right. I'll bite, you crusty bastard...

Who are you? *And what do you want?*

Well, today I'm that *bad man*...the one with death in his eyes, and the best weapons money can buy...

And I want noth more tha to watch someone bleed out

And why in the world would you think *what you want* has anything to do with what you're *going* to get?

Who lives their life thinking that way?

Haven't you been listenin', son?

I do.

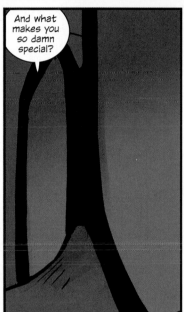

And what makes you so damn special?

I am **the** law.

And today -- come hell or high water -- I will deliver justice to the Chosen, John Freeman.

Wait...you're here to kill the Crown Prince?

I am.

Well, that's interesting. Maybe next time lead with that. Come on...

Follow me.

HE **STOLE** WHAT WAS
YOURS AND GAVE IT TO YOUR
ENEMY.

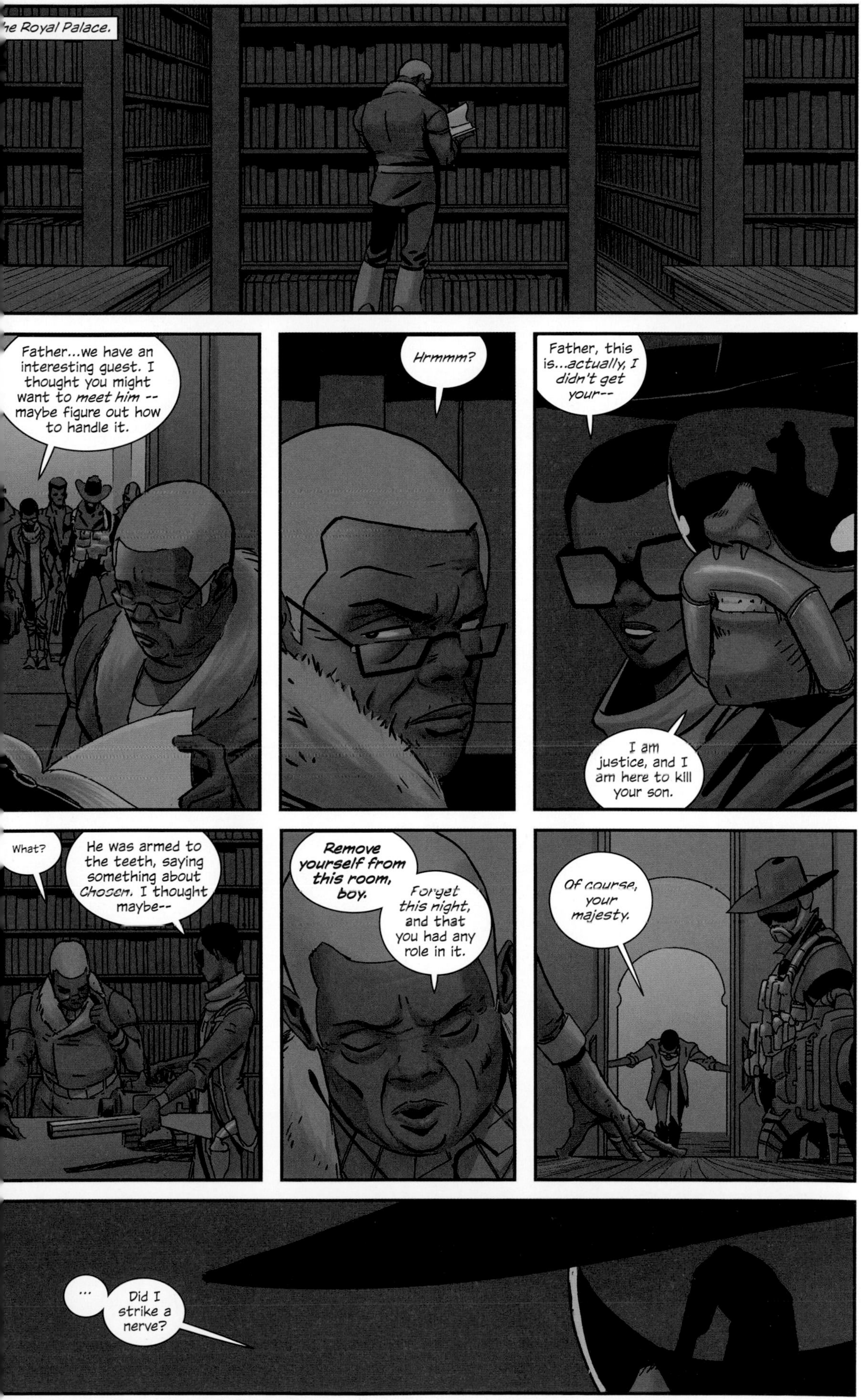

he Royal Palace.
Father...we have an interesting guest. I thought you might want to meet him -- maybe figure out how to handle it.
Hrmmm?
Father, this is...actually, I didn't get your--
I am justice, and I am here to kill your son.
What?
He was armed to the teeth, saying something about Chosen. I thought maybe--
Remove yourself from this room, boy.
Forget this night, and that you had any role in it.
Of course, your majesty.
...
Did I strike a nerve?

You seem to believe there are things that happen in my kingdom of which I am unaware -- *I assure you...that's not the case.*

I know of my son's *dalliances.* I know the danger they pose.

You talk like this is a complex thing, when it's really pretty simple.

Yes, *it is.* Simple in the way that you longer have a nation -- simple in th way you think I won't do everything my power to protect mine.

You're not the law here, ranger...you're just the face of it.

I am the law.

Judge, jury, and *all* that follows.

Then do something about it...or get outta my way!

...

You're asking me for *justice* -- and I cannot give you that. So let me offer you *mercy* instead.

Take your life. My guards will escort you from the palace, but leave the weapons behind.

That's fine. Keep the guns. I've got more.

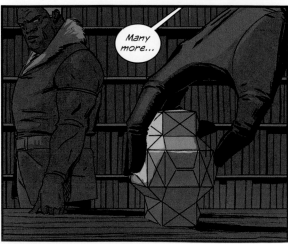

Many more...

As many as you have sons.

HOW CAN YOU CALL
THIS **MAN** YOUR **SON?**

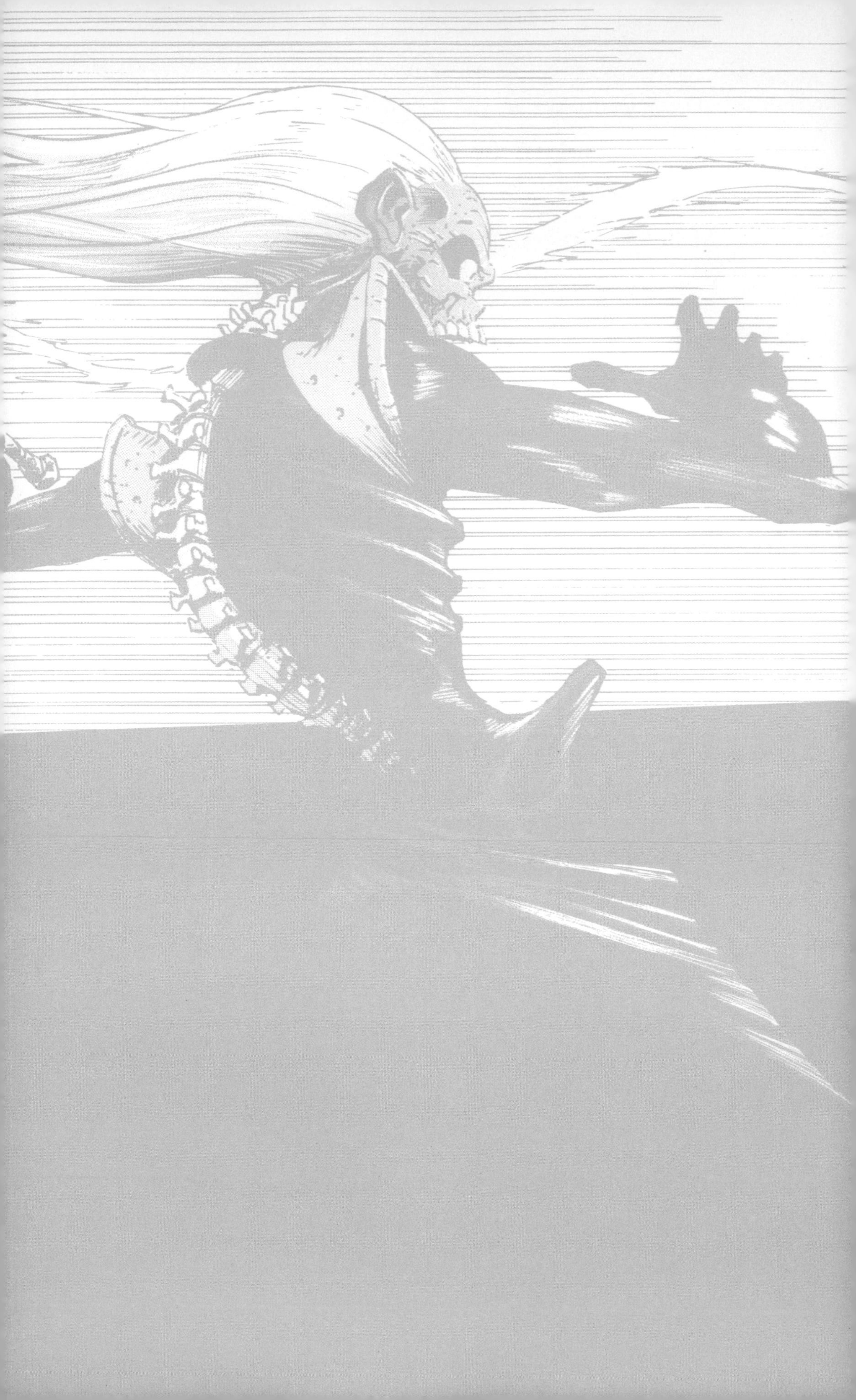

THIRTY-EIGHT:
THE **ONCE** AND
FUTURE KING

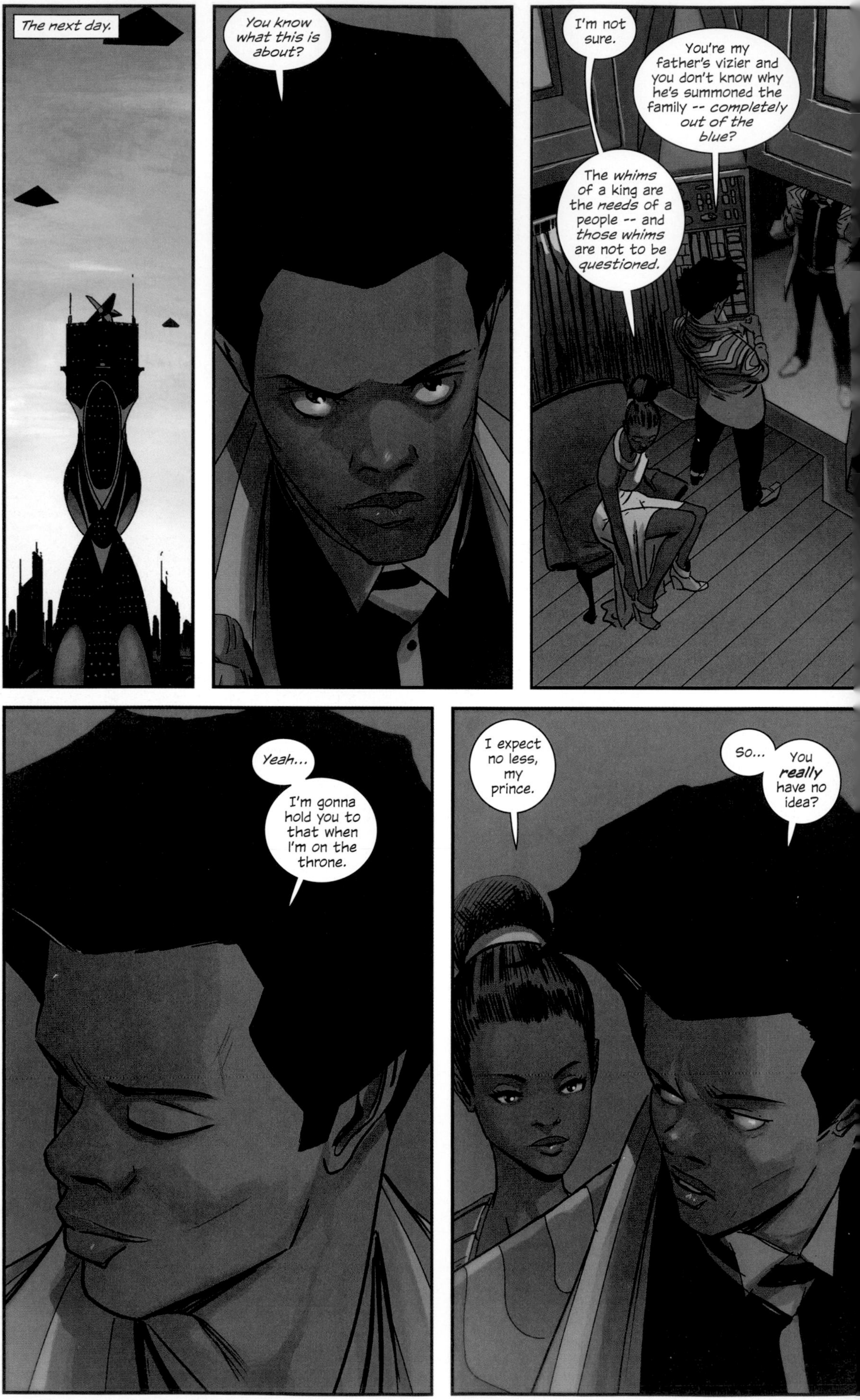
The next day.
You know what this is about?
I'm not sure.
You're my father's vizier and you don't know why he's summoned the family -- completely out of the blue?
The whims of a king are the needs of a people -- and those whims are not to be questioned.
Yeah...
I'm gonna hold you to that when I'm on the throne.
I expect no less, my prince.
So...
You really have no idea?

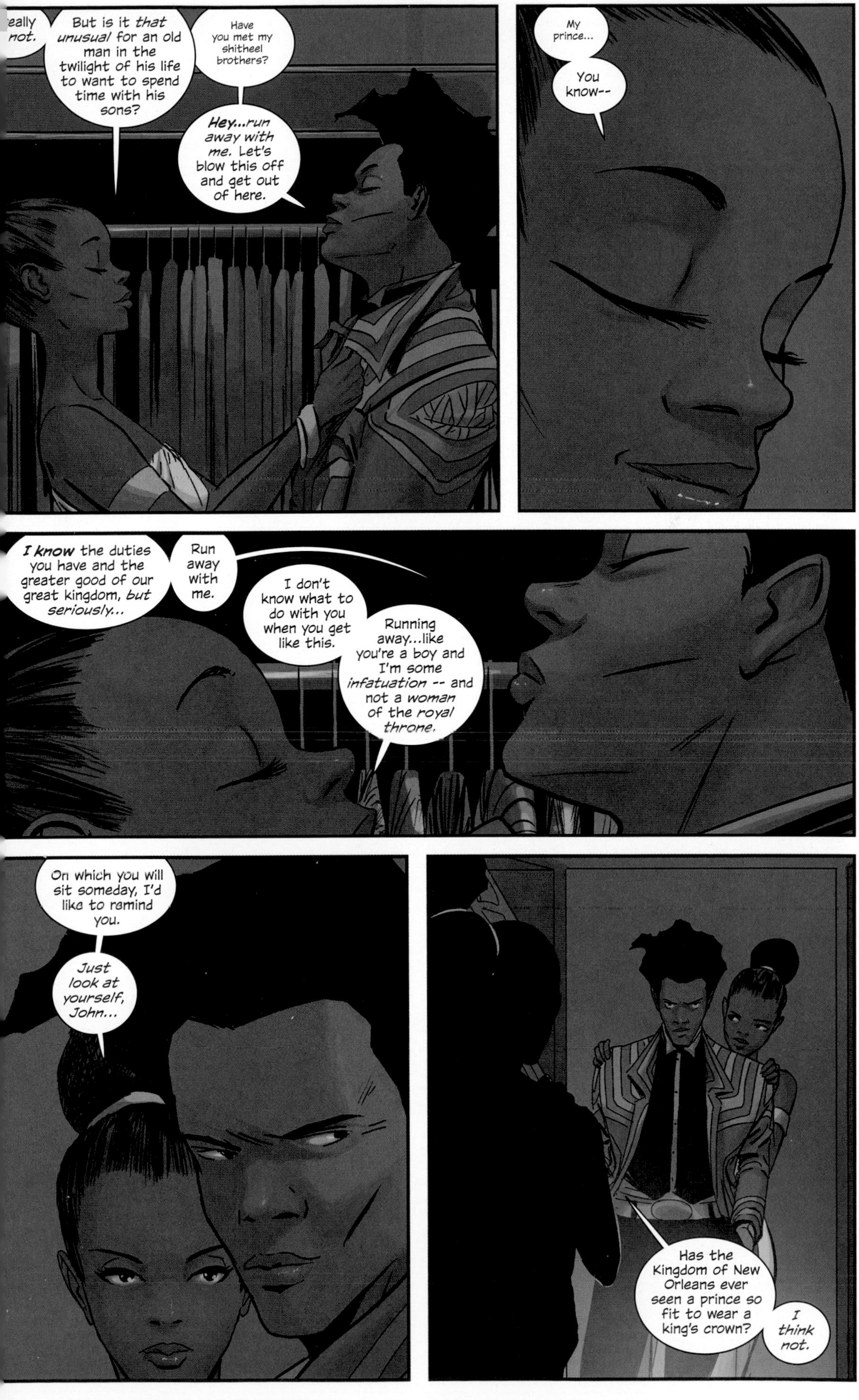

eally not.
But is it *that unusual* for an old man in the twilight of his life to want to spend time with his sons?
Have you met my shitheel brothers?
Hey...run away with me. Let's blow this off and get out of here.
My prince...
You know--
I know the duties you have and the greater good of our great kingdom, *but seriously...*
Run away with me.
I don't know what to do with you when you get like this.
Running away...like you're a boy and I'm some *infatuation* -- and not a *woman* of the *royal throne.*
On which you will sit someday, I'd like to remind you.
Just look at yourself, John...
Has the Kingdom of New Orleans ever seen a prince so fit to wear a king's crown?
I think not.

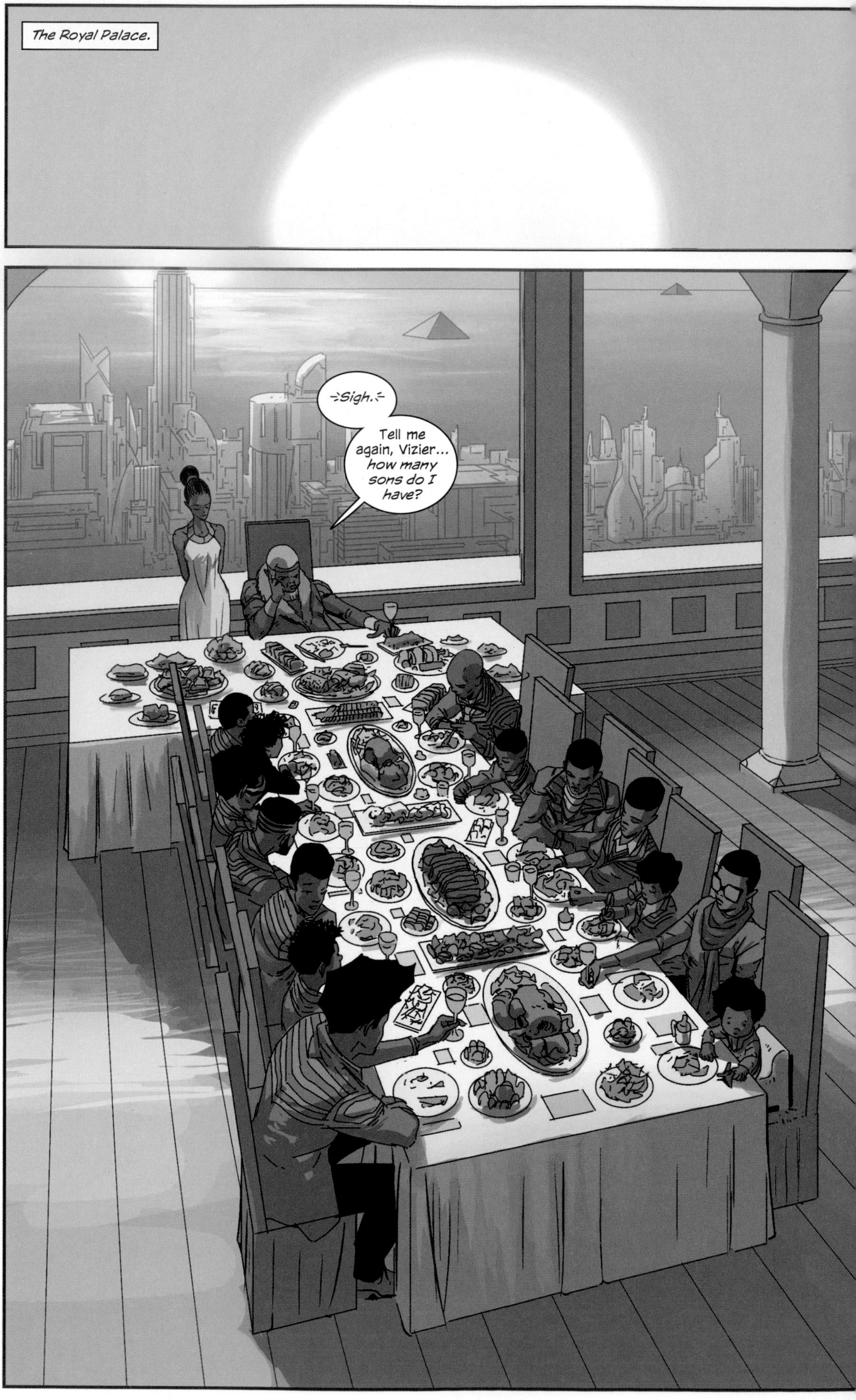
The Royal Palace.
-Sigh.-
Tell me again, Vizier... how many sons do I have?

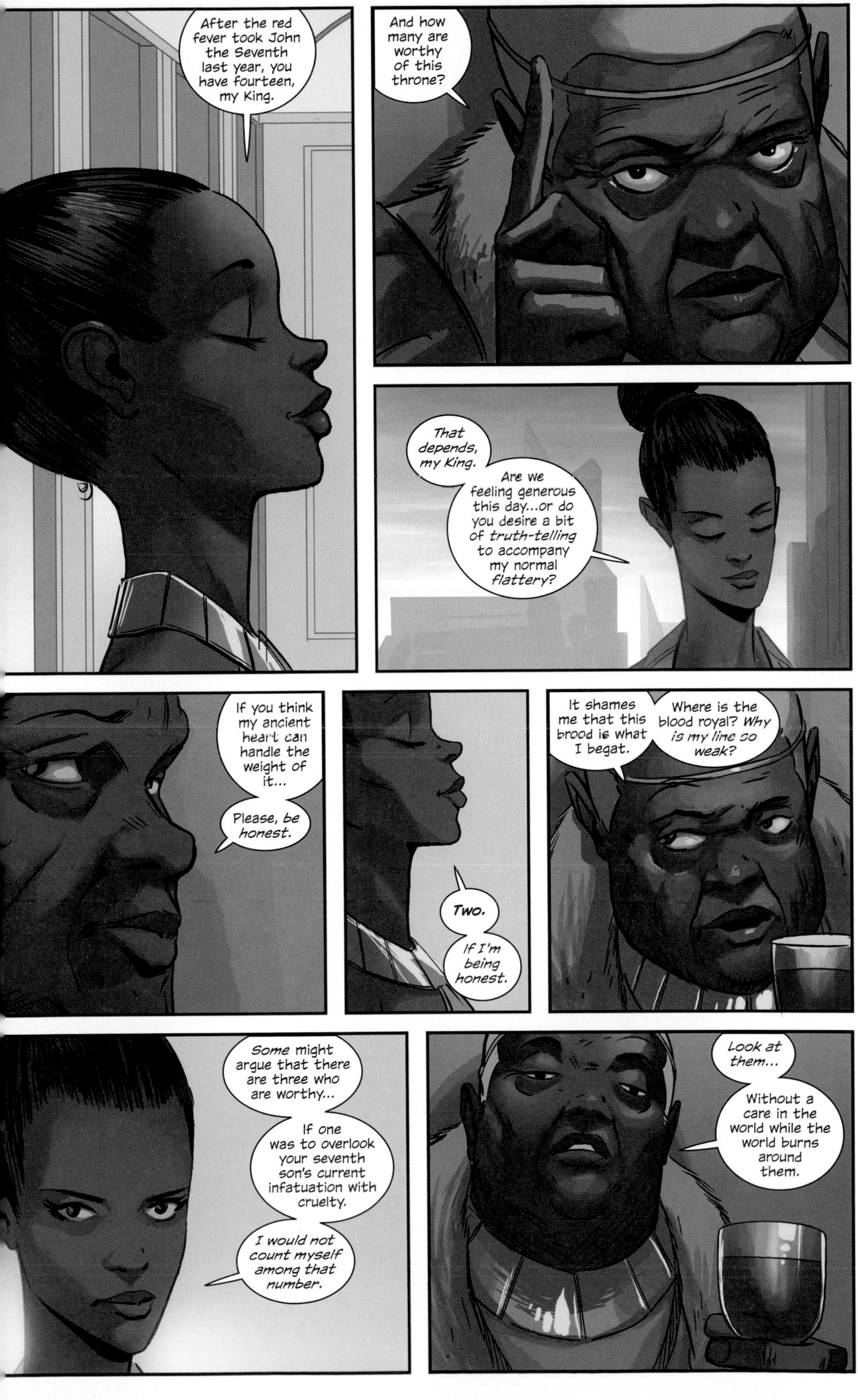
After the red fever took John the Seventh last year, you have fourteen, my King.
And how many are worthy of this throne?
That depends, my King.
Are we feeling generous this day...or do you desire a bit of truth-telling to accompany my normal flattery?
If you think my ancient heart can handle the weight of it...
Please, be honest.
Two.
If I'm being honest.
It shames me that this brood is what I begat.
Where is the blood royal? Why is my line so weak?
Some might argue that there are three who are worthy...
If one was to overlook your seventh son's current infatuation with cruelty.
I would not count myself among that number.
Look at them...
Without a care in the world while the world burns around them.

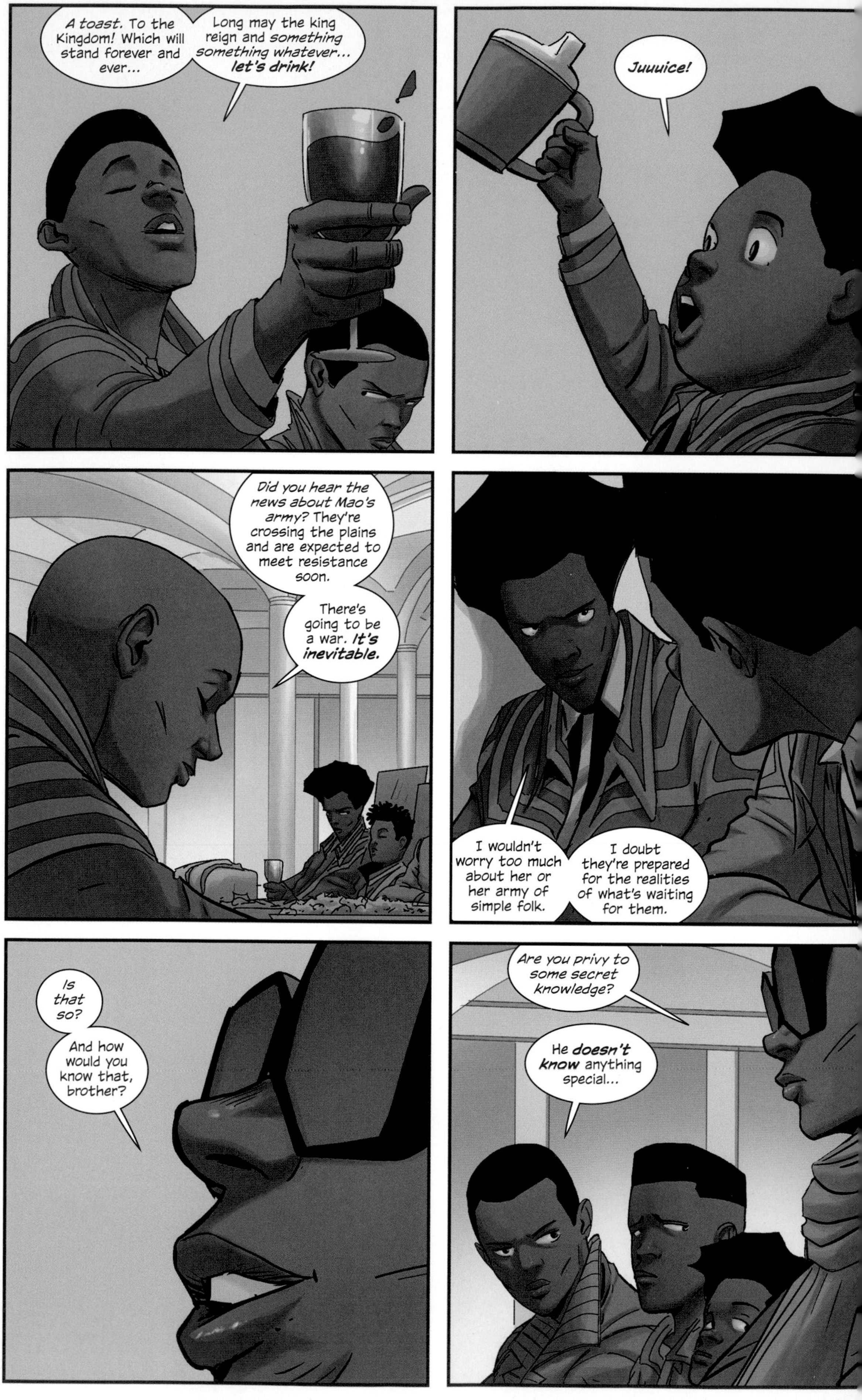
A toast. To the Kingdom! Which will stand forever and ever...
Long may the king reign and something something whatever... let's drink!
Juuuice!
Did you hear the news about Mao's army? They're crossing the plains and are expected to meet resistance soon.
There's going to be a war. It's inevitable.
I wouldn't worry too much about her or her army of simple folk.
I doubt they're prepared for the realities of what's waiting for them.
Is that so?
And how would you know that, brother?
Are you privy to some secret knowledge?
He doesn't know anything special...

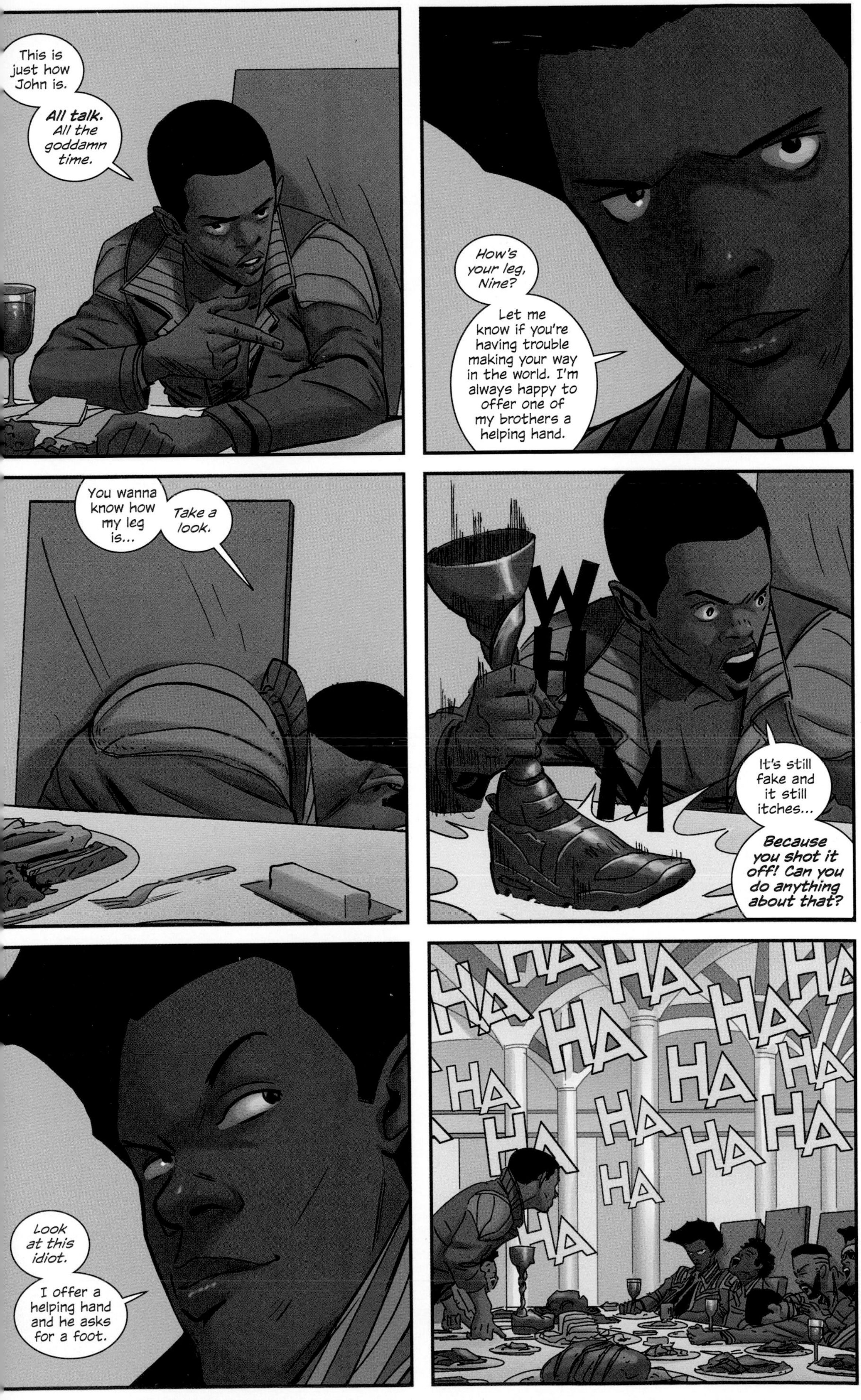
This is just how John is.
All talk. All the goddamn time.
How's your leg, Nine?
Let me know if you're having trouble making your way in the world. I'm always happy to offer one of my brothers a helping hand.
You wanna know how my leg is...
Take a look.
WHAM
It's still fake and it still itches...
Because you shot it off! Can you do anything about that?
Look at this idiot.
I offer a helping hand and he asks for a foot.
HA HA HA HA HA HA HA HA HA HA HA HA HA HA HA HA HA HA HA HA HA

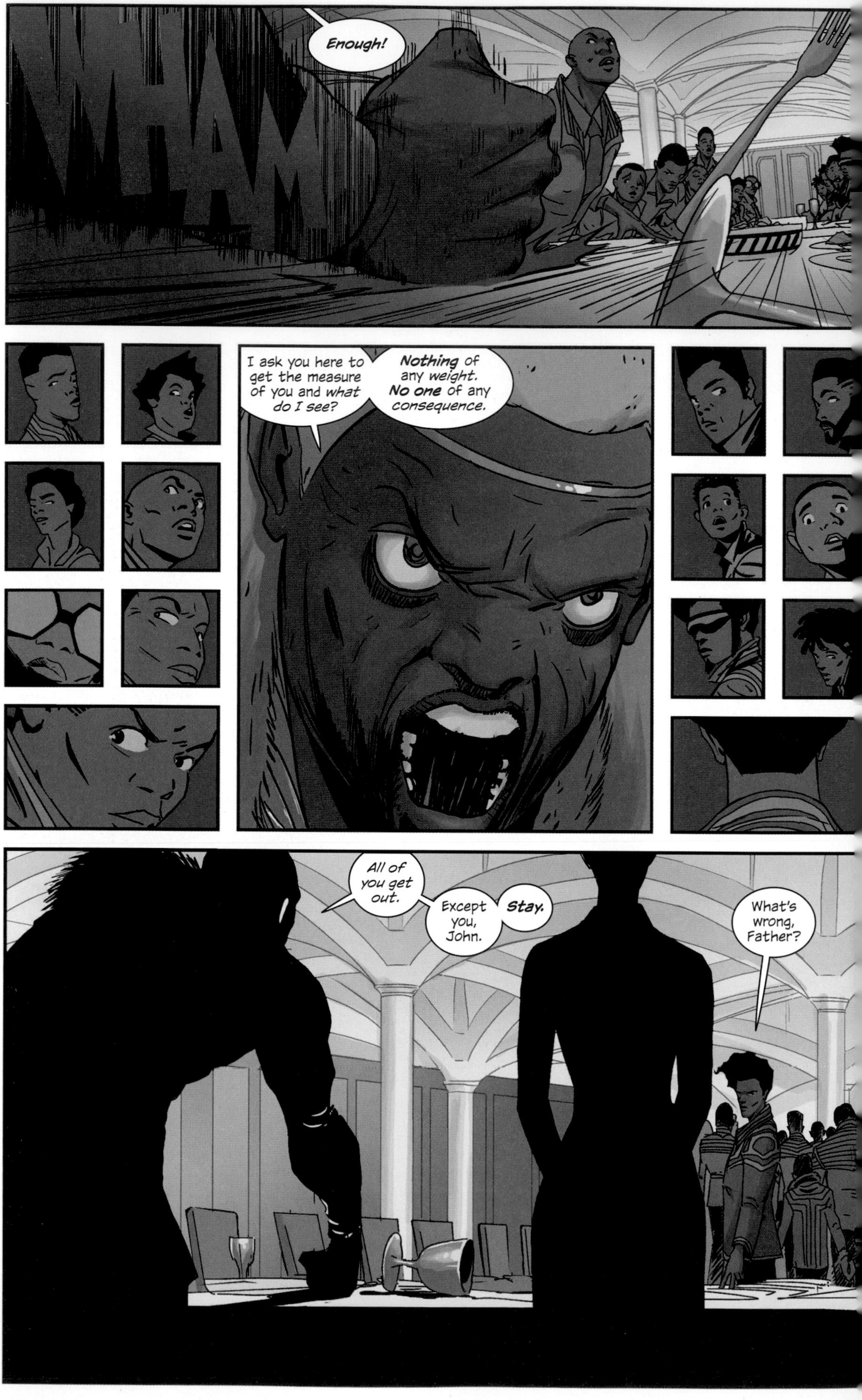
WHAM
Enough!
I ask you here to get the measure of you and what do I see?
Nothing of any weight. No one of any consequence.
All of you get out.
Except you, John.
Stay.
What's wrong, Father?

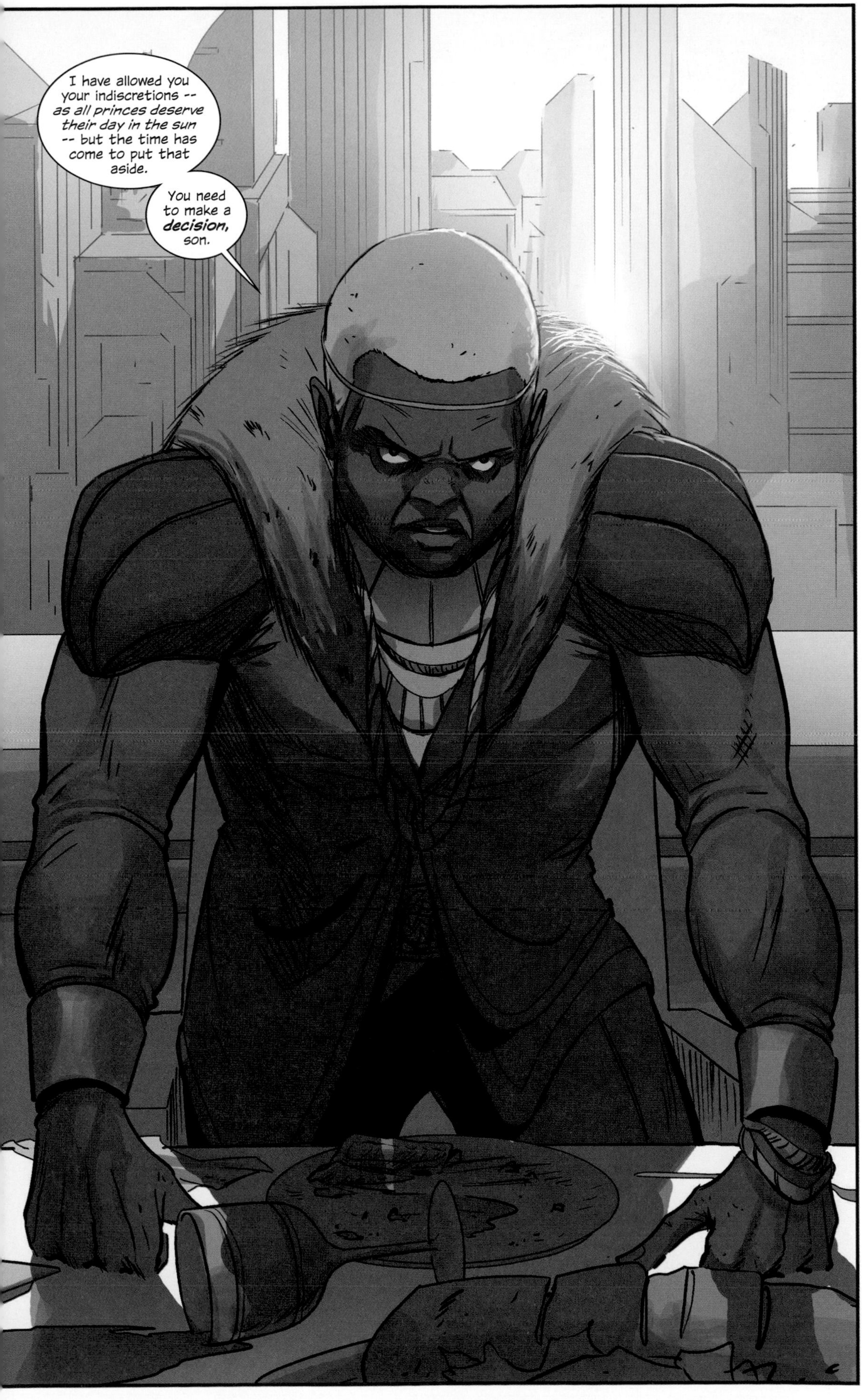
I have allowed you your indiscretions -- *as all princes deserve their day in the sun* -- but the time has come to put that aside.
You need to make a ***decision,*** son.

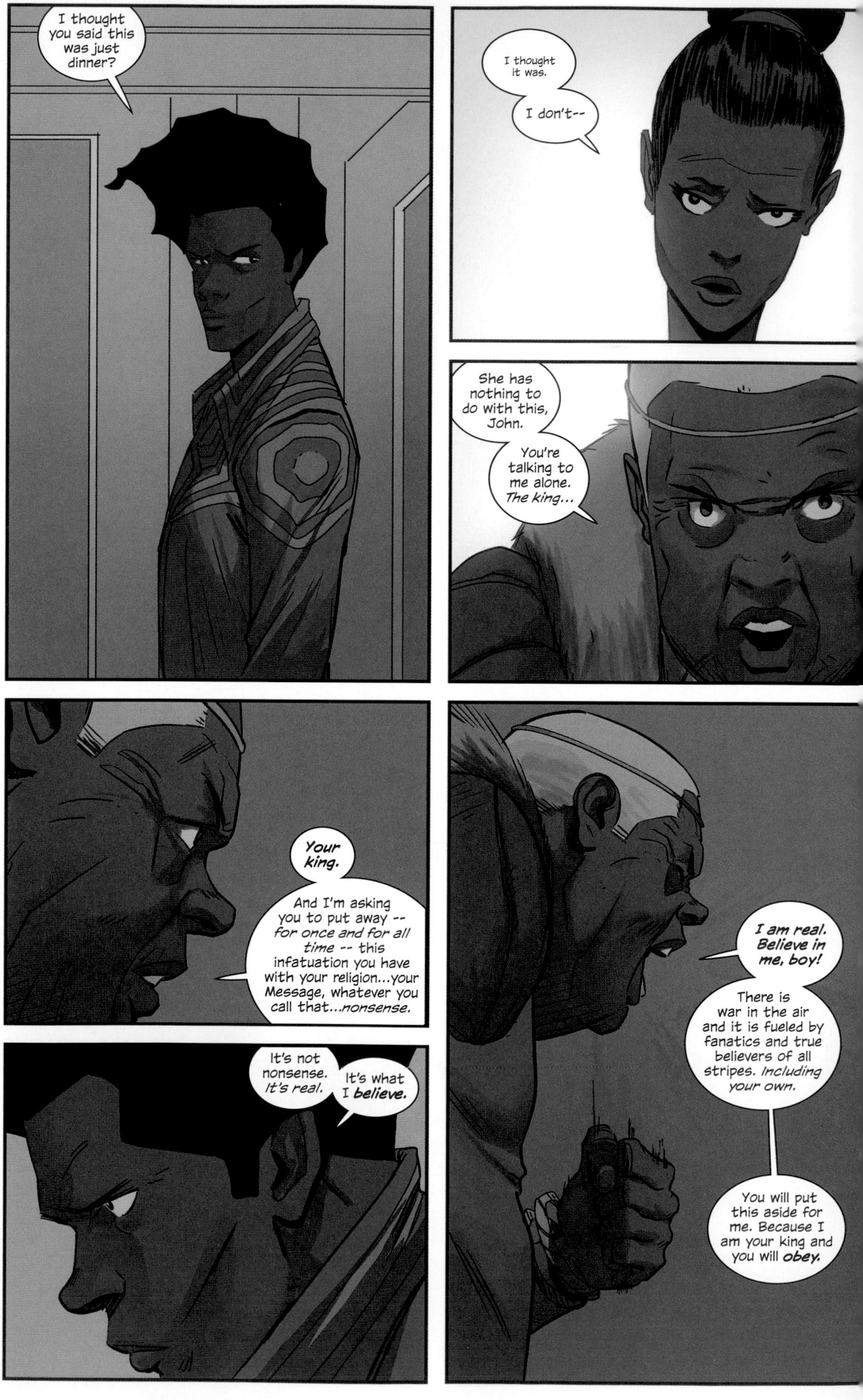
I thought you said this was just dinner?
I thought it was.
I don't--
She has nothing to do with this, John.
You're talking to me alone. *The king...*
Your king.
And I'm asking you to put away -- *for once and for all time* -- this infatuation you have with your religion...your Message, whatever you call that...*nonsense.*
It's not nonsense. *It's real.*
It's what I ***believe.***
I am real. Believe in me, boy!
There is war in the air and it is fueled by fanatics and true believers of all stripes. *Including your own.*
You will put this aside for me. Because I am your king and you will ***obey.***

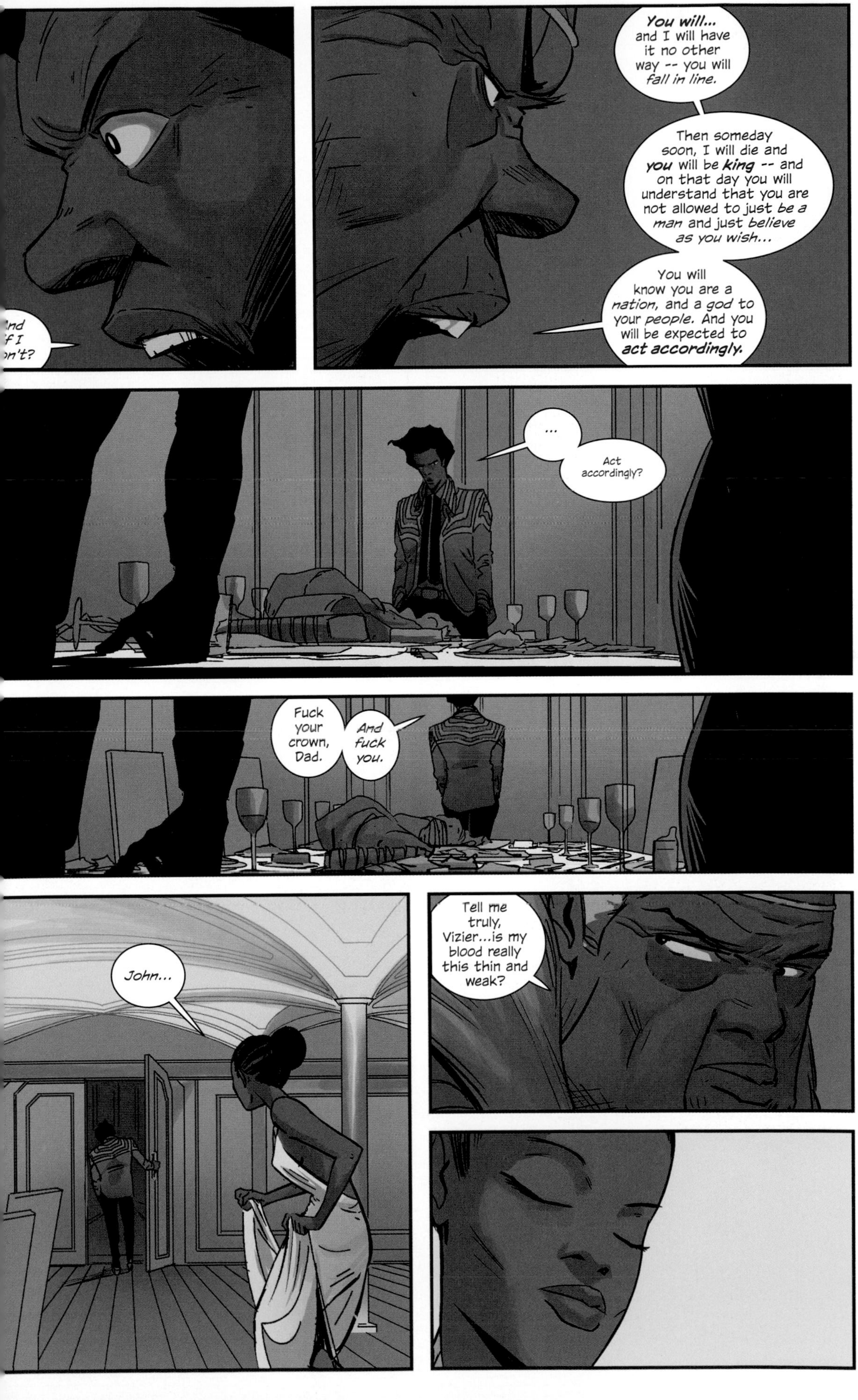

...nd ...f I ...n't?
You will... and I will have it no other way -- you will fall in line.
Then someday soon, I will die and you will be king -- and on that day you will understand that you are not allowed to just be a man and just believe as you wish...
You will know you are a nation, and a god to your people. And you will be expected to act accordingly.
...
Act accordingly?
Fuck your crown, Dad.
And fuck you.
John...
Tell me truly, Vizier...is my blood really this thin and weak?

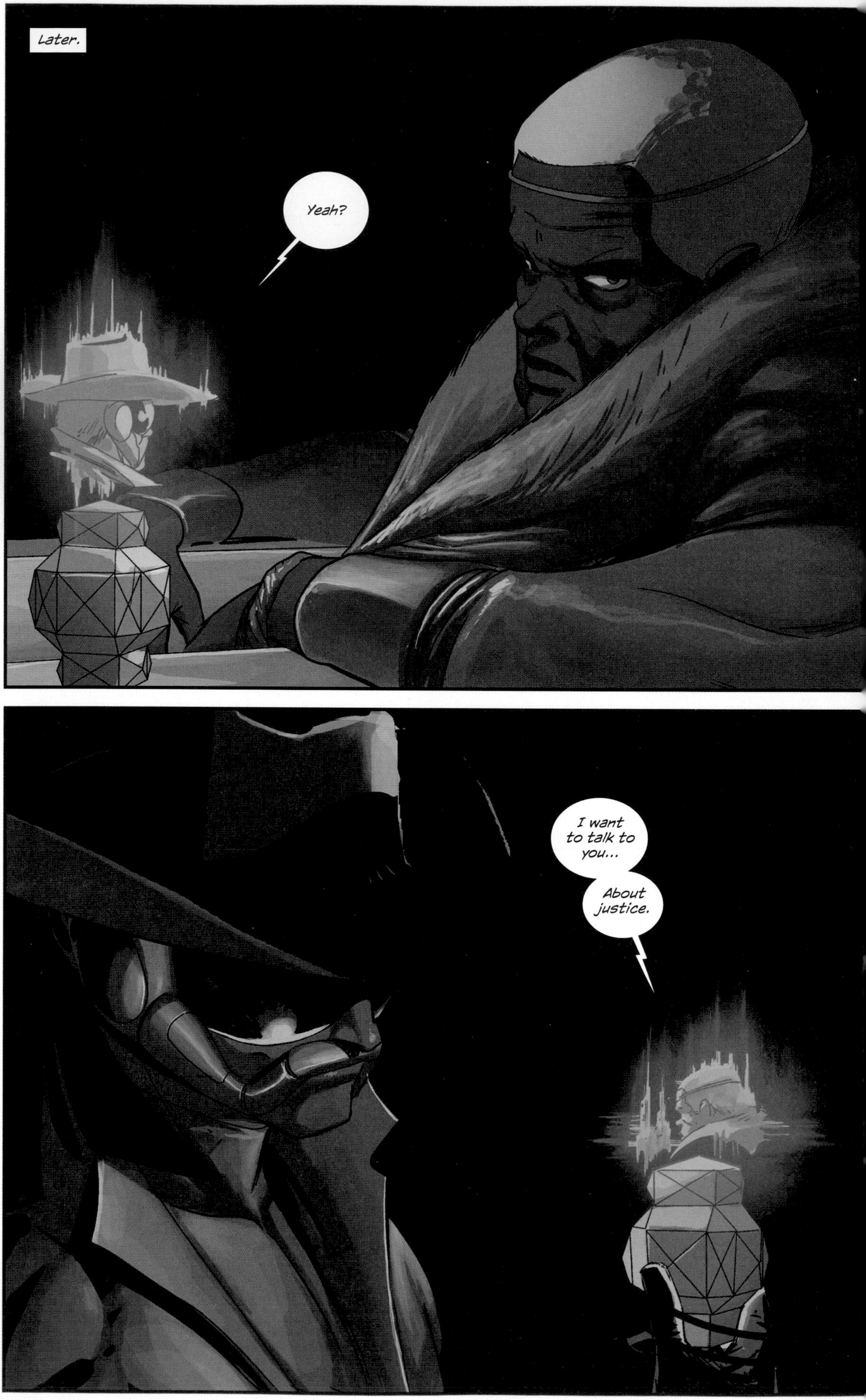
Later.
Yeah?
I want to talk to you...
About justice.

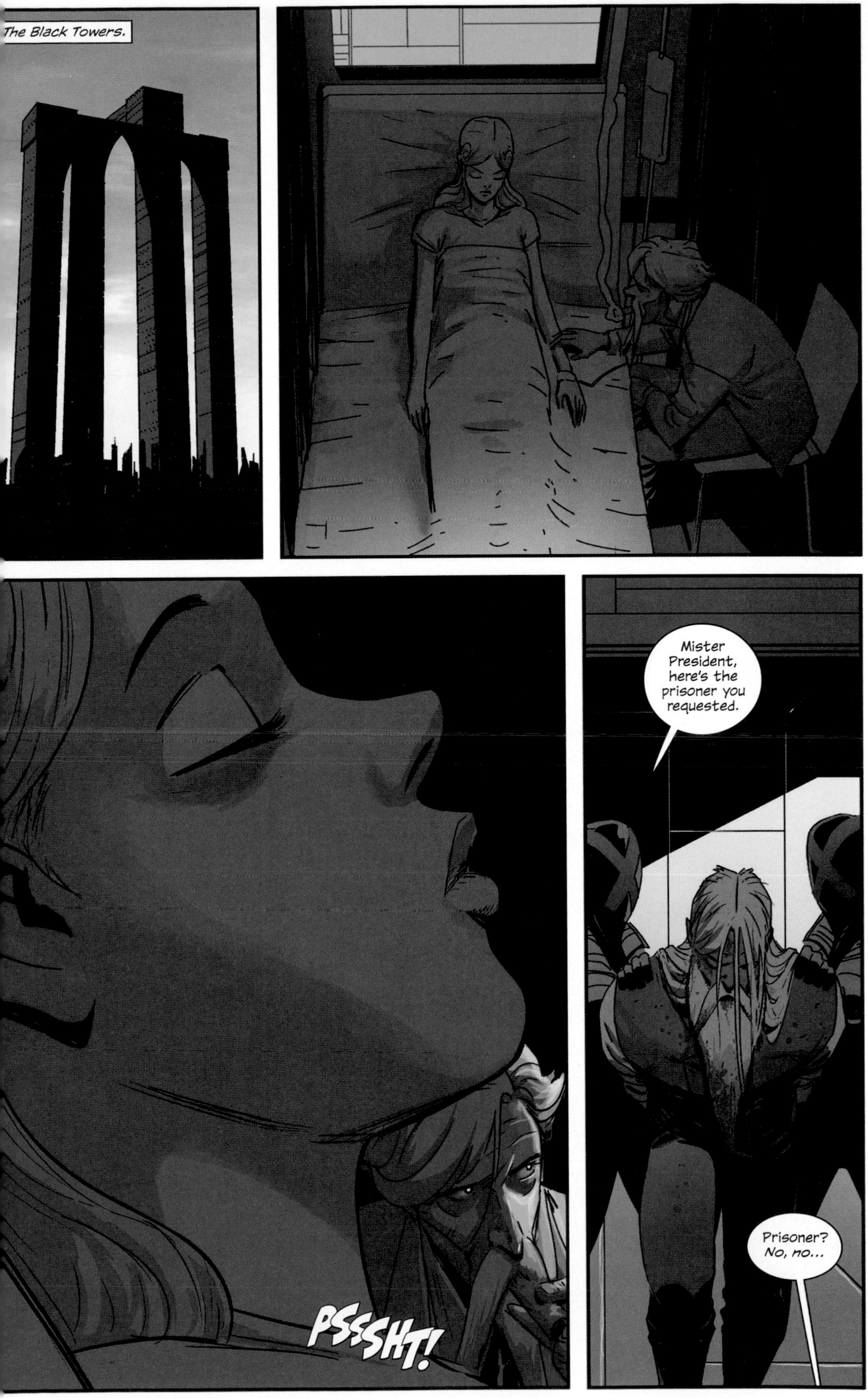
The Black Towers.
Mister President, here's the prisoner you requested.
PSSSHT!
Prisoner? No, no...

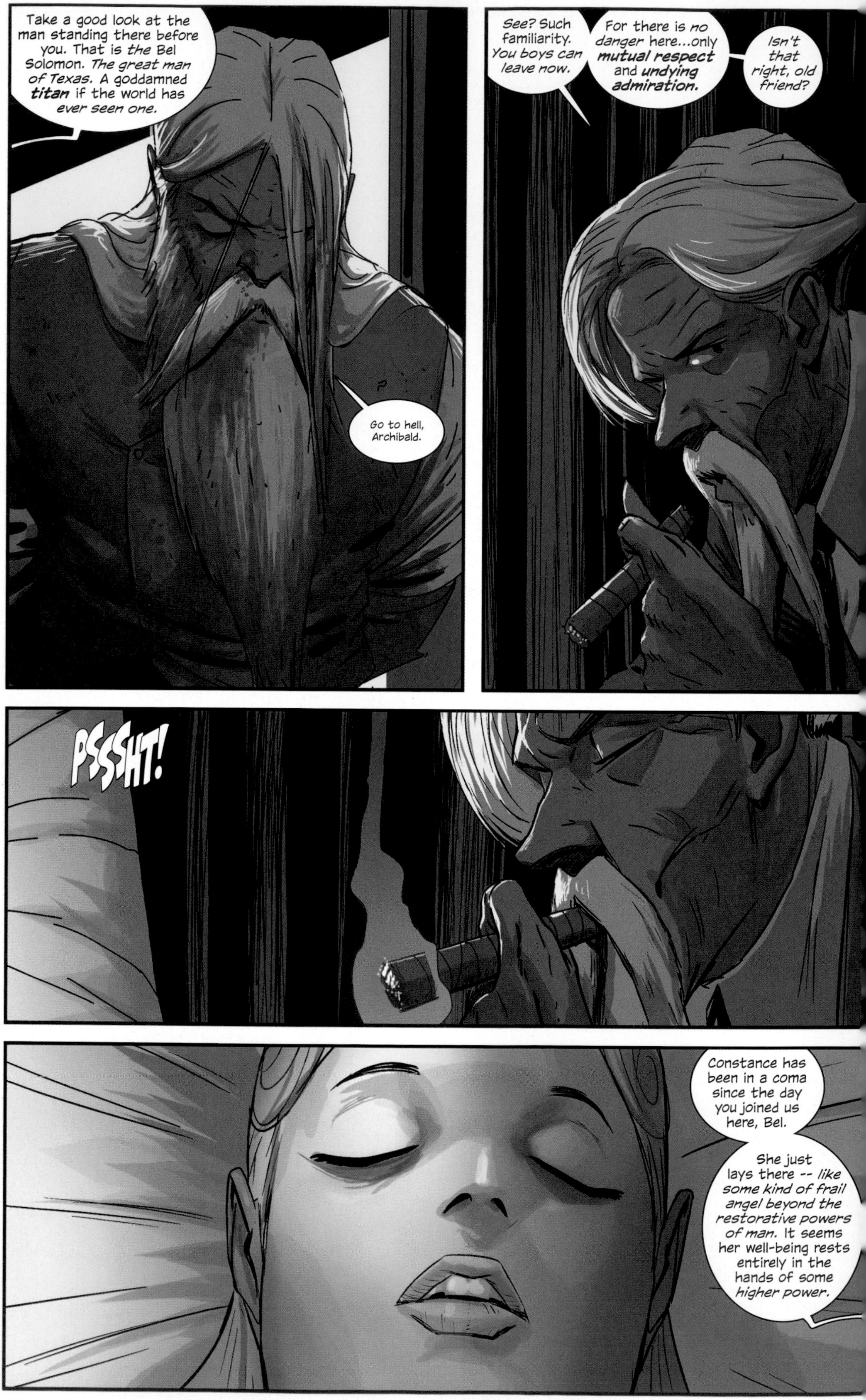
Take a good look at the man standing there before you. That is *the* Bel Solomon. *The great man of Texas.* A goddamned **titan** if the world has *ever seen one.*
Go to hell, Archibald.
See? Such familiarity. *You boys can leave now.*
For there is *no danger* here...only **mutual respect** and **undying admiration.**
Isn't that right, old friend?
PSSSHT!
Constance has been in a coma since the day you joined us here, Bel.
She just lays there -- *like some kind of frail angel beyond the restorative powers of man.* It seems her well-being rests entirely in the hands of some *higher power.*

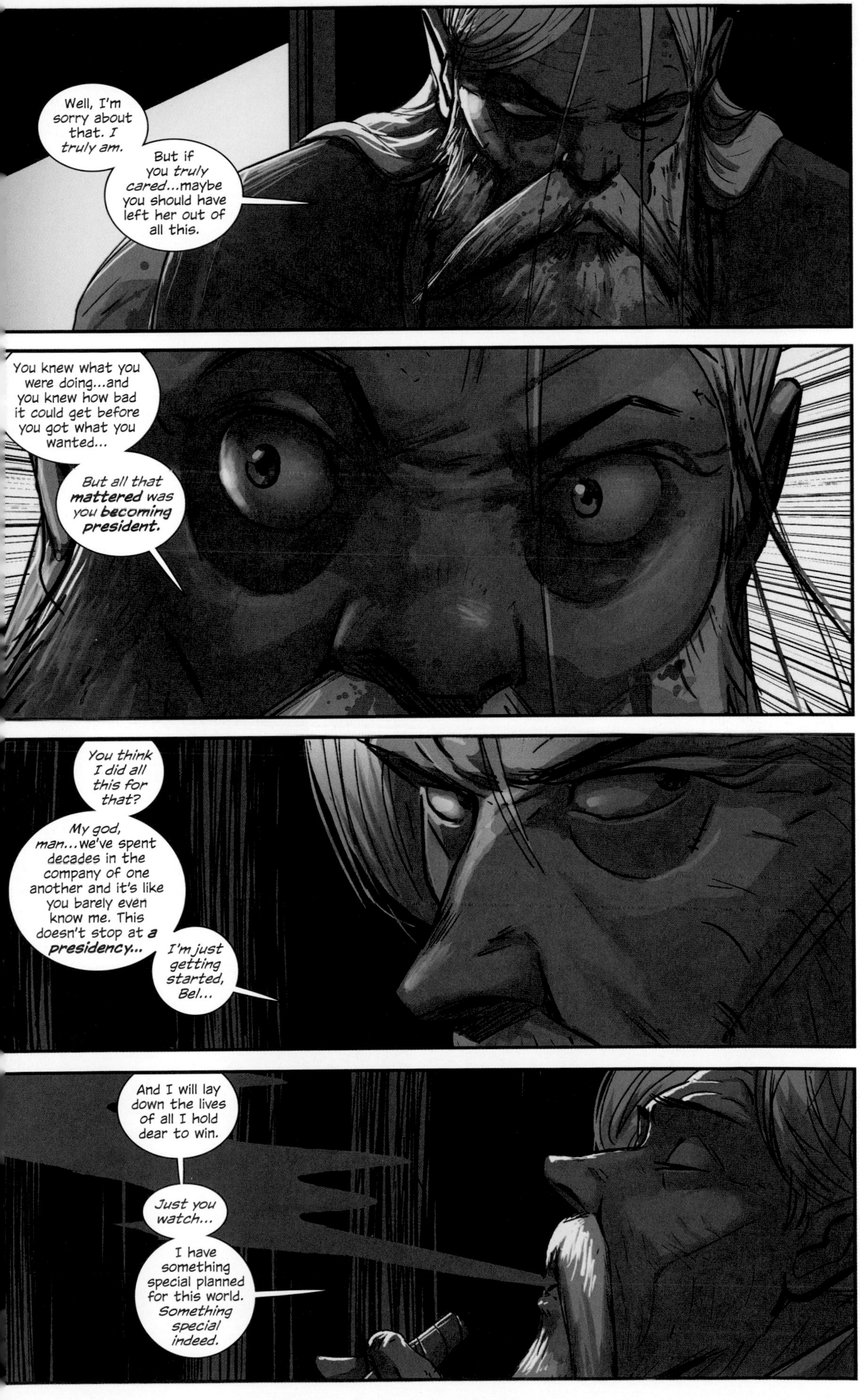
Well, I'm sorry about that. *I truly am.*
But if you *truly cared*...maybe you should have left her out of all this.
You knew what you were doing...and you knew how bad it could get before you got what you wanted...
But all that ***mattered*** *was you* ***becoming president.***
You think I did all this for that?
My god, man...we've spent decades in the company of one another and it's like you barely even know me. This doesn't stop at ***a presidency...***
I'm just getting started, Bel...
And I will lay down the lives of all I hold dear to win.
Just you watch...
I have something special planned for this world. *Something special indeed.*

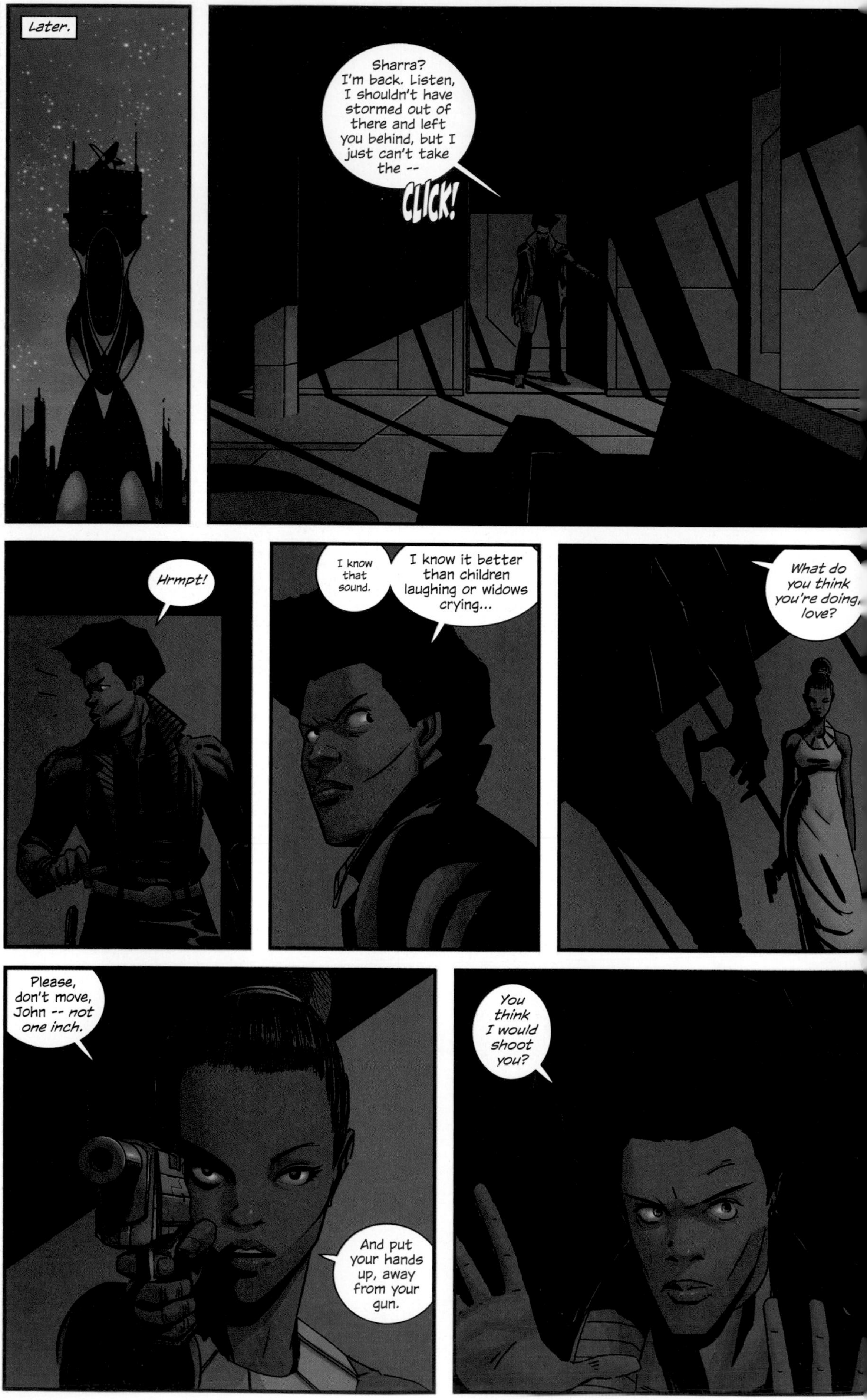
Later.
Sharra? I'm back. Listen, I shouldn't have stormed out of there and left you behind, but I just can't take the --
CLICK!
Hrmpt!
I know that sound.
I know it better than children laughing or widows crying...
What do you think you're doing, love?
Please, don't move, John -- not one inch.
And put your hands up, away from your gun.
You think I would shoot you?

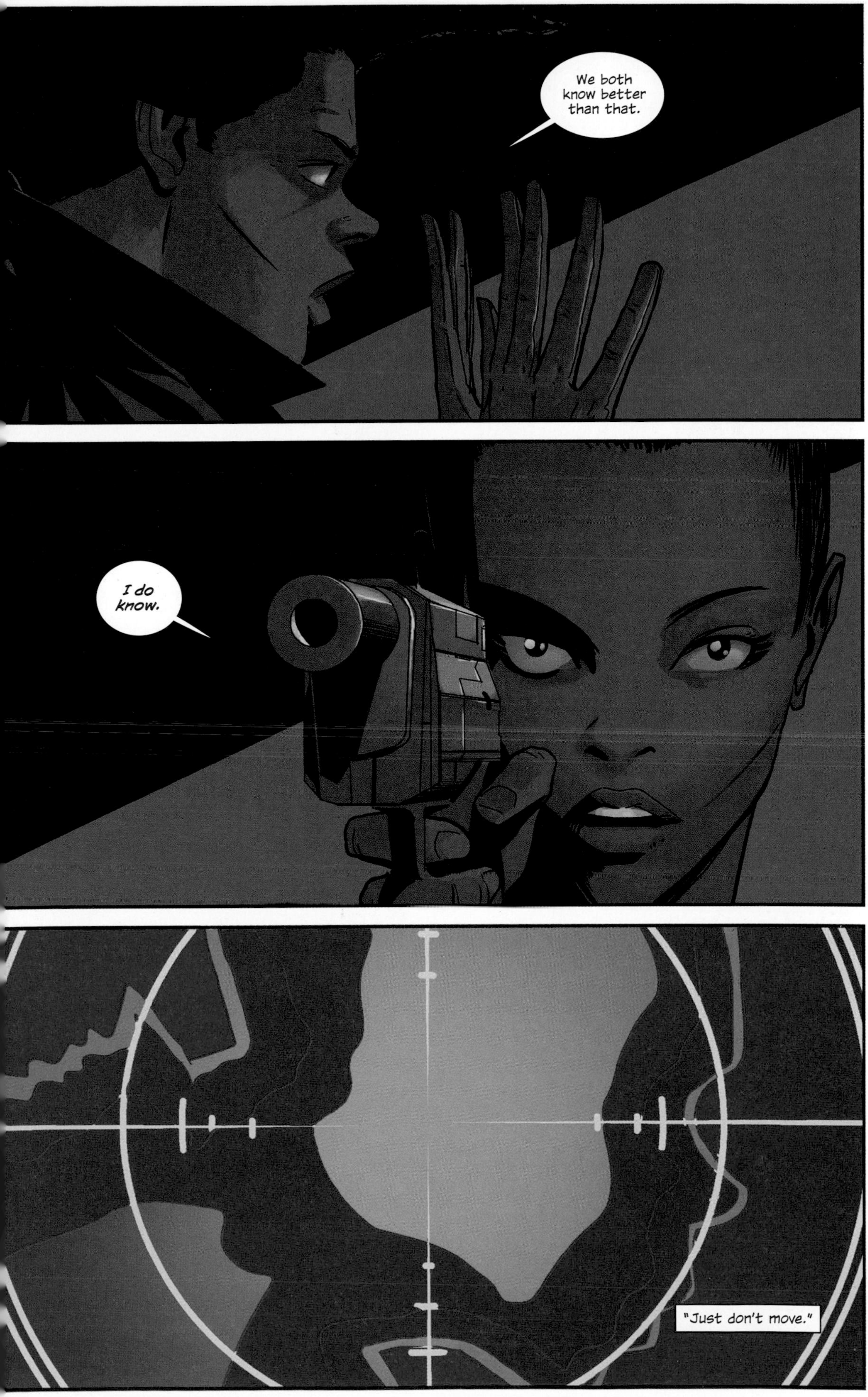
We both know better than that.
I do know.
"Just don't move."

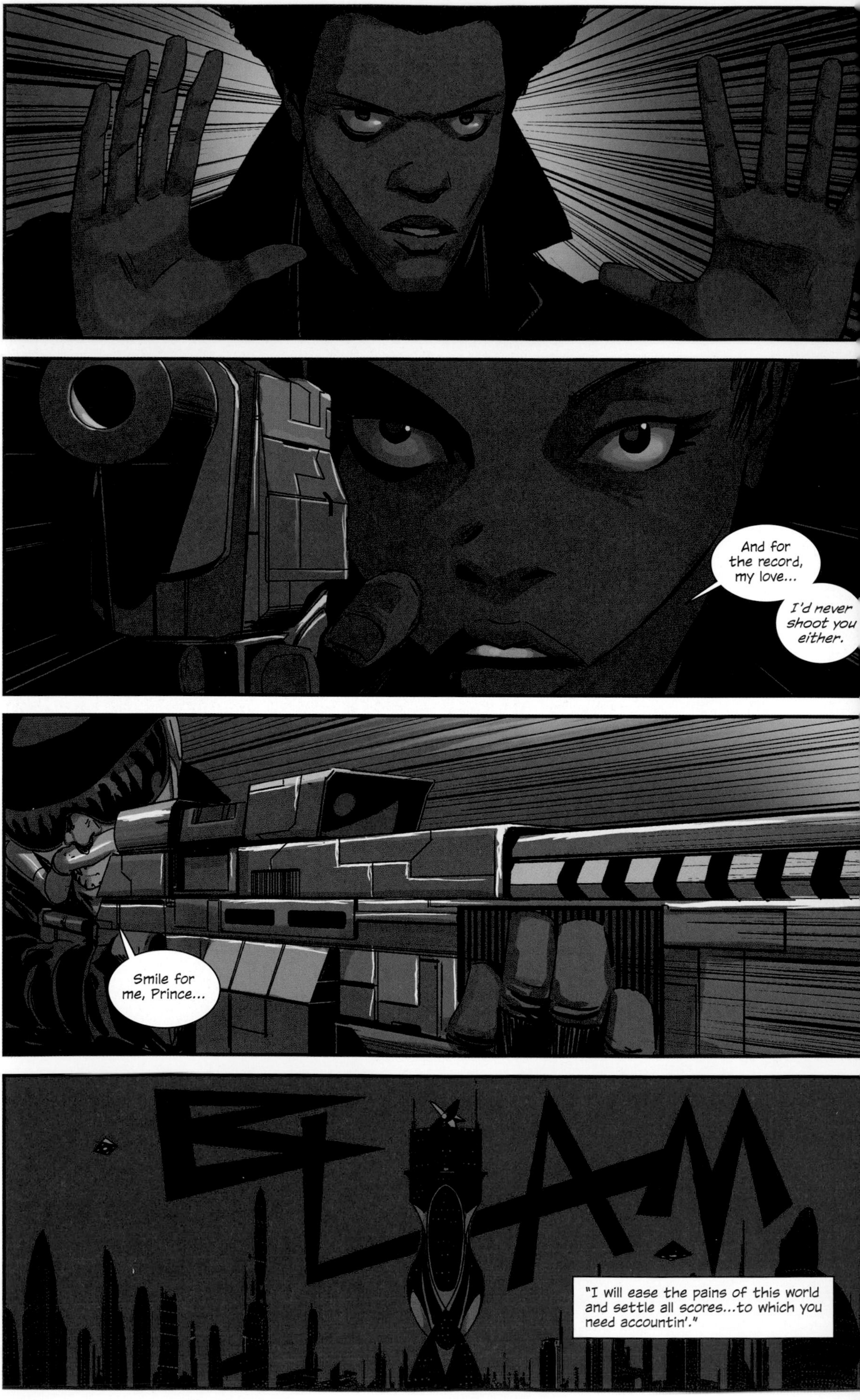
And for the record, my love...
I'd never shoot you either.
Smile for me, Prince...
BLAM
"I will ease the pains of this world and settle all scores...to which you need accountin'."

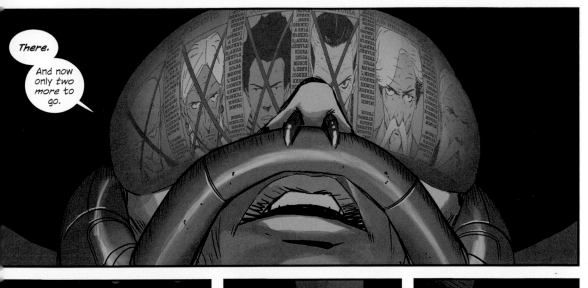

There.

And now only *two* more to go.

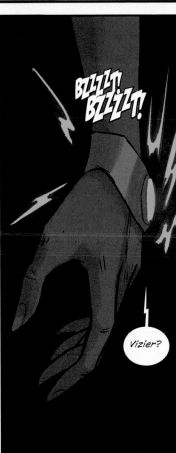

BZZZT! BZZZT!

Vizier?

Yes, my King?

Tell me...

How many sons do I have?

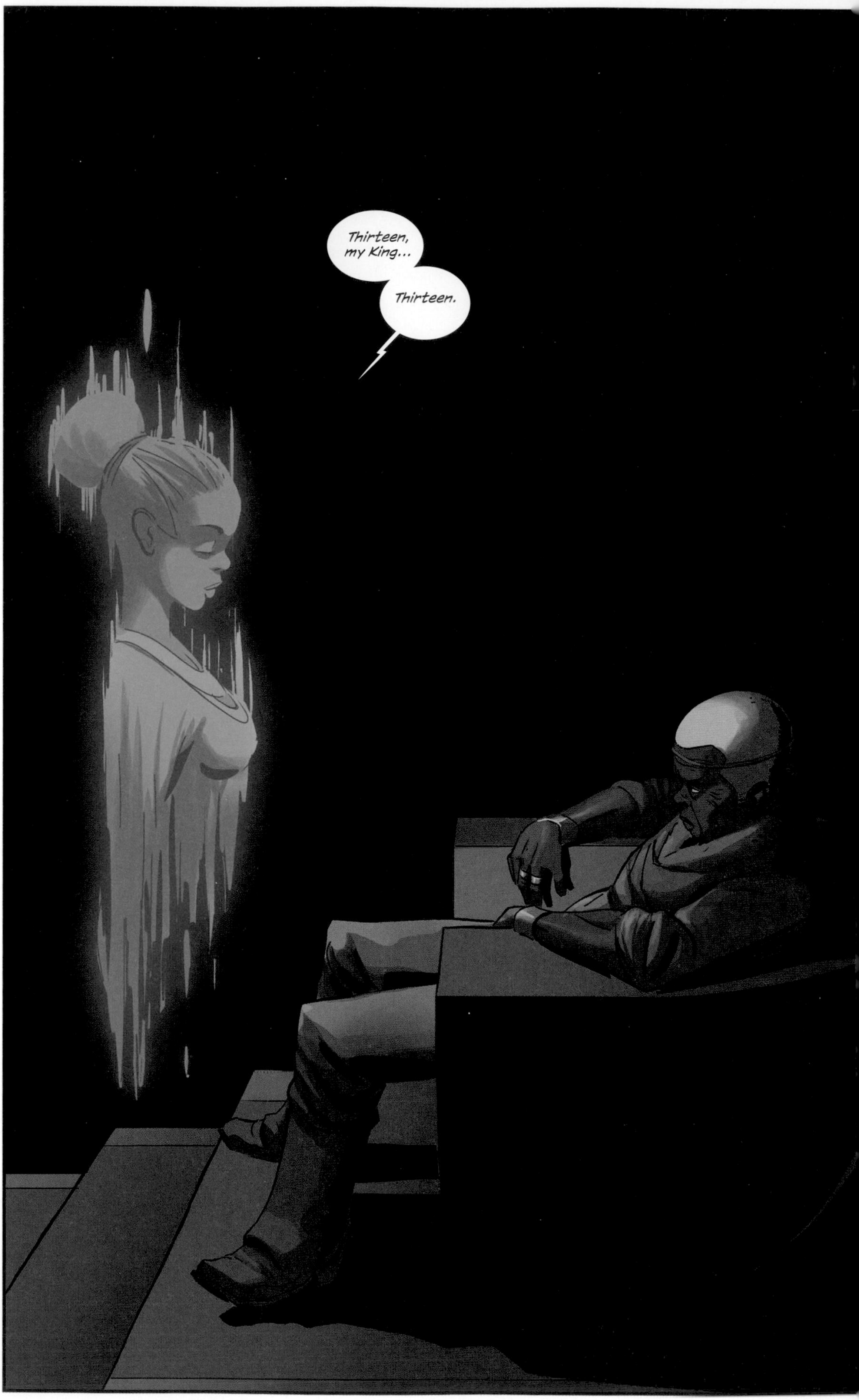
Thirteen, my King...
Thirteen.

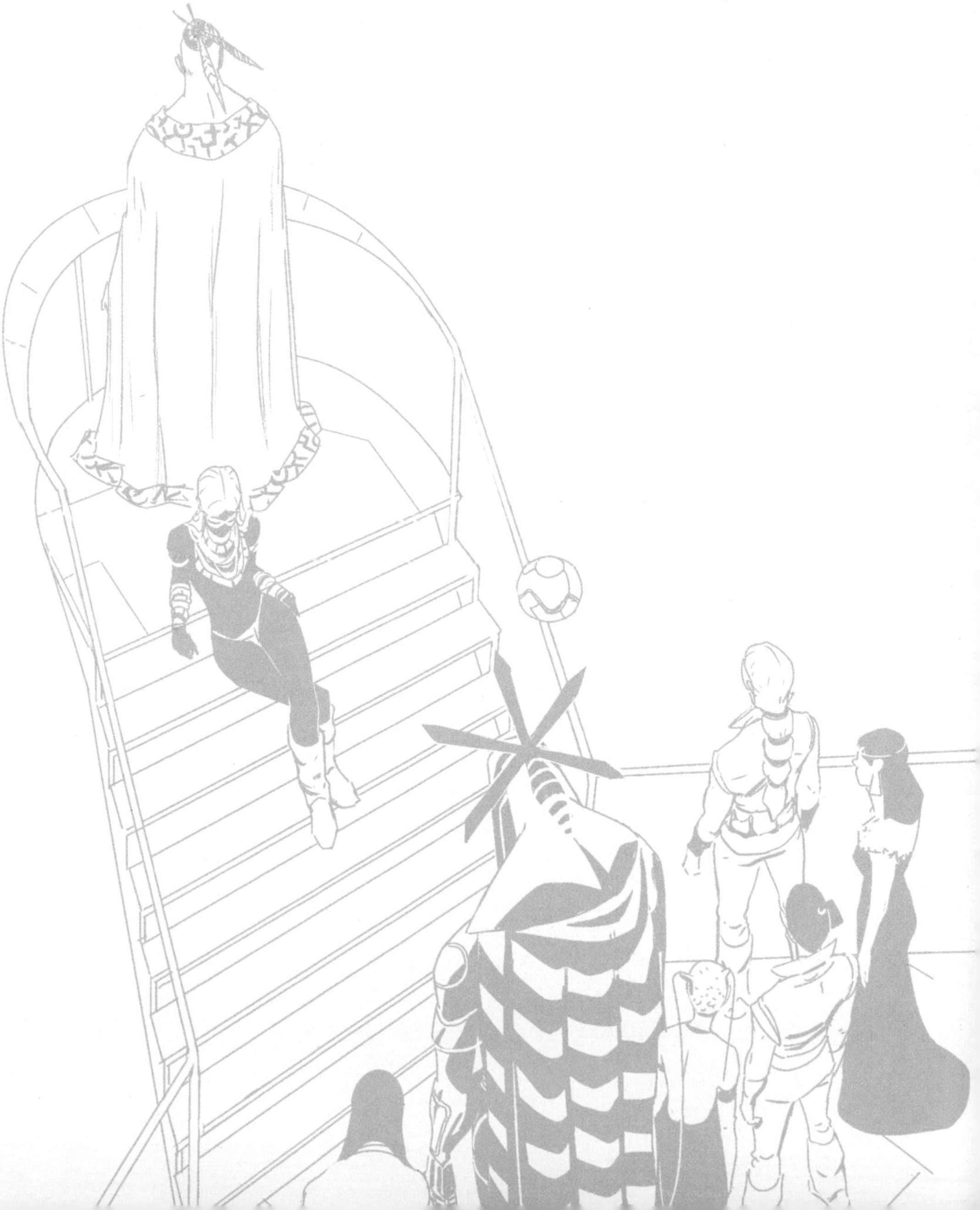

ALL MEN TELL **LIES.**
THESE ARE A **FEW** OF
THEM.

Jonathan Hickman is the visionary talent behind such works as the Eisner-nominated **NIGHTLY NEWS**, **THE MANHATTAN PROJECTS** and **PAX ROMANA**. He also plies his trade at MARVEL working on books like **FANTASTIC FOUR** and **THE AVENGERS**.

His twin brother, Marc, was just named the PGA caddie of the year.

Jonathan lives in South Carolina except when he doesn't.

You can visit his website: ***www.pronea.com***, or email him at: ***jonathan@pronea.com***.

·

Nick Dragotta's career began at Marvel Comics working on titles as varied as **X-STATIX, THE AGE OF THE SENTRY, X-MEN: FIRST CLASS, CAPTAIN AMERICA: FOREVER ALLIES** and **VENGEANCE.**

In addition, Nick is the co-creator of **HOWTOONS,** a comic series teaching kids how to build things and explore the world around them. **EAST OF WEST** is Nick's first creator-owned project at Image.